Boeing 747.

Queen of the Skies

Farewell From The Flight Deck.
By Owen Zupp

Boeing 747. Farewell to the Queen is one of nine books by Owen Zupp. His first book, 'Down to Earth', was published in 2006 by Grub Street (UK). An award-winning aviation writer, his work has been featured in magazines across the globe including Fly Past (UK), Airliner World (UK), Aviation History (US), Plane & Pilot (US), Global Aviator (South Africa), Australian Flying and Australian Aviation. Owen has won Australasian Aviation Press Club awards and is a commercial pilot with more than thirty years' experience.

www.owenzupp.com

OWEN ZUPP

BOEING 747.

FAREWELL FROM THE FLIGHT DECK.

OWEN ZUPP

Published by
There and Back
P.O. Box 747
Bowral NSW 2576
Australia

National Library of Australia cataloging-in-publication entry
Creator: Zupp, Owen, author. 1964-
Title: Boeing 747. Queen of the Skies. Farewell from the Flight Deck.
Subjects: Aeroplanes. Piloting – biography. Air pilots – Australia.
ISBN 998-0-9946038-6-9

Read more by Owen Zupp.
Boeing 747. Reflections from the Flight Deck. (eBook and Paperback)
'50 Tales of Flight' (Paperback and eBook)
'50 More Tales of Flight' (Paperback and eBook)
Without Precedent: Commando, Fighter Pilot and the true story of Australia's first Purple Heart (Paperback and eBook)
'Down to Earth' A Fighter Pilot's Experiences of surviving Dunkirk, the Battle of Britain, Dieppe, and D-Day. (Grub Street Publishing. 2007)
'Solo Flight' One Pilot's Aviation Adventure around Australia (Paperback and eBook)
The Practical Pilot (Paperback and eBook)
"Do it Like a Pilot. Leadership, Communication, Teamwork, and Management Skills from Ground Up." (Paperback and eBook)

Author's Website. www.owenzupp.com

Cover Image: Liam Ireland.

Back Cover Image: Seth Jaworski.

For Kirrily.

Amazing wife, mother, pilot and my best friend.
All my love, now and always

CONTENTS

About This Book.

F ollowing my return from the final flight of the last Qantas Boeing 747, I was approached by many readers to expand upon my original book, "Boeing 747. Reflections from the Flight Deck". This book is the answer to that request from those who also treasured the "Queen of the Skies".

This is a personal account of my experiences from training through to my two terms as flight crew on this wonderful aircraft. Divided into four parts, this book offers insights into the aircraft, the air routes, the international destinations and significant events, good and bad, that occurred along the way. Some recollections are technical, some are observations and some are personal.

The 747 entered my life as a total surprise and twice represented major turning points in my career. If it is possible to be indebted to an aeroplane, then I certainly owe the Boeing 747 for making my life richer.

This book is a tribute to the aircraft that changed the world.

PREFLIGHT.

That I ever had the privilege of operating the Boeing 747 was a twist of fate. The airline for which I was flying collapsed, leaving me with 10,000 hours in my logbook, but very few prospects. Fortunately, I was given the opportunity to fly for the Australian national carrier, Qantas, and that's where I met the 747.

From that first preflight inspection, I was in awe of the aircraft. The fact that it had almost single-handedly shrunk the world and that it was engineered to span oceans comfortably at Mach 0.86 and yet routinely slip across the airfield fence on arrival at 140 knots. I vividly recall standing at the wingtip and realising that it almost extended as far back as the rearmost door. The angle of sweep on the wing was akin to an F-86 Sabre fighter jet! It was fast, it was big and it was versatile and over the years used for every task imaginable – from piggy-backing the Space Shuttle to Air Force One and so, so much more.

Over the years, I have flown a range of aircraft, but the 747 will always hold a special place. As both a pilot and an aviation writer I have been extremely fortunate to witness a number of very special flights beyond the normal air routes. Such flights as a charter to Antarctica, the frozen continent, and Cathay's first freighter flight using the Boeing 747-8F. And of course, the final farewell of the last Qantas 747 after nearly half a century of service.

In this book, it is a privilege to be able to share some of those flights with you. Some offer insight behind the scenes, while others are more reflective of the majesty with which the 747 crossed the sky.

It is no wonder that she is warmly referred to as the "Queen of the Skies".

Owen Zupp

PART ONE
AN INTRODUCTION
TO ROYALTY.

CHAPTER ONE
THE END.

The runway had loomed large in the windscreen of the 747 countless times before – but this was something special. After nearly half a century of service with Qantas, the graceful giant descended towards its final reunion with the earth under the hands of a captain with a parallel history.

In his 26,000 hours of flight time, Ewen Cameron had spent all but 1,500 hours on the flight deck of a Qantas Boeing 747. Now, he nudged the thrust levers and guided the control column with a familiar touch, through the invisible bubbles of disturbed, convective air rising from the Mojave Desert.

Ahead lay 12,000 feet of runway and one last landing. Beyond this touchdown, both man and machine would be retired. A fate that was to be shared by other members of the crew. For now, any sense of reflection or emotion was tucked away. There was only a focus on the task at hand.

He scanned the instruments inside and the world outside of the flight deck.

Airspeed.

Aim Point.

Perspective. High or low?

The flight across from Los Angeles had only been a short one

- twenty minutes in the air. Even so, the farewell had been memorable. Fire trucks had sprayed water cannons across the bow and a police escort had accompanied Qantas Flight Number QF7474 along the taxiway. Kind words had been exchanged with Air Traffic Control and, as helicopters hovered, the photographers hoped to grab that perfect shot.

A wave of the wings had been plain to see from the ground before the aircraft rolled gracefully to the right and set course. She slipped over the ridgeline and the descent was interrupted by a light aircraft ahead, perhaps also hoping to grab a perfect shot. If so, they undoubtedly would have captured the moment when Ewen disengaged the autopilot, stopped the descent, and wheeled the 747 through a gentle 360-degree orbit to remain clear of any other aircraft.

Free to continue, the Mojave Air and Space Port then passed beneath as the aircraft joined the circuit to land. Below, the "boneyard" of discarded airliners seemed to gaze up at the new arrival. Their coloured fins and white fuselages contrasted against the rusty desert floor. From the air, they appeared to be scattered at random, as if tipped out of some giant's bag of toys. For the moment, this 747 was still at home in the air.

Airspeed.

Aim Point.

Perspective. High or Low?

"Five Hundred" the radio altimeter called out the height above the ground.

"Stable" Captain Fitzgerald responded from the right seat.

Not much further now.

Nearly there.

CHAPTER TWO
An Unlikely Meeting.

Personally, I had never imagined that I would ever fly a 747, nor had I harboured any deep desire to do so. My airline career had seen me flying for a domestic airline, Ansett Australia, with relatively short sectors each day and with multiple take-offs and landings. It was a busy life, but enjoyable, and the thought of twelve or more hours at a time cooped up inside an aeroplane, didn't appeal to me. In fact, I vividly recall a long 5-hour flight between two capital cities and subsequently wondering how the international pilots could do it. Anyway, it wasn't my concern as I was a domestic airline pilot with a job-for-life,

A few weeks later, I was unemployed.

My airline had collapsed in the early hours of the Friday morning after the attacks of 9/11 and I was left standing on the footpath, unable to enter the passenger terminal. Finally, a security guard granted me access to clean out my things before escorting me back to the footpath. With 10,000 hours of flight time and a licence full of qualifications, I had been discarded without notice. It wasn't a high point. Still, as pilots, we are trained to act and that's what I did.

Instead of operating the 6 am, Boeing 737 service to Melbourne, I drove my car and parked outside a flying school at a regional airport. There I waited for their doors to open to ask if they needed another flight instructor. There was a chill in the air and the wind whipped around my car's aerial, providing an occasional whistle. With my seat reclined and my eyes skyward, I was deciding between going to sleep or contemplating the reality of being nearly forty years of age and washed up as an airline pilot. At that very moment, a razor-sharp contrail came into my line of sight.

To this day, I don't know if the aircraft was a 747, although I highly suspect that it was.

It was a four-engined aircraft by the broad path that its multiple white trails cut. Perhaps this was another omen? The day I was first accepted into an airline I had parked behind a car with "737" on its number plate just before I received the phone call. Either way, those four white lines set to the backdrop of the bluest of skies gave my spirits a much-needed lift.

The next few months saw me earn an income by coaching sport and teaching aviation theory at the school where I had waited that morning. It was a positive experience that took my mind off my airline career and gave me a reason to rise each day with a purpose. All the while I was applying for employment as a pilot, as were all my former workmates.

Then, within a week, the tide turned. A range of opportunities arose and at the top of the list was an invitation to be interviewed by Qantas, Australia's national airline. If successful, it would mean starting at the bottom of their seniority list as a junior pilot but that didn't matter. To be flying again, with Qantas and still living in Australia ticked all of the boxes for my wife, Kirrily, and me.

Kirrily had joined Qantas as a pilot years earlier and was now a First Officer on the Boeing 767. Her insight into the recruitment process was invaluable as I sat through the psychometric testing and then the face-to-face interview. Across the table, Captains Phil Patterson and Greg Fitzgerald peppered me with a range of questions, both technical and of a general nature. At one point, Captain Fitzgerald pressed me on the neatness of my logbook, querying if I'd rewritten it for the interview. To answer, I drew out five other logbooks from my briefcase and opened them. I've always been particular about logging my flights, seeing my logs as a record of my aviation journey.

For a recruitment process that was not known for its pace, surprisingly, I was called back to be assessed in the simulator within days. Driving past the landing threshold of Sydney Airport's Runway 16 Right, Airport Drive changes its name to Qantas Drive as the entrance to the Arthur Baird Jet Base draws near. As aircraft passed low overhead in their final phase of flight, the unmistakable red fins of the Boeing 747s dominated the view. A mixture of the older models and the newer "400 Series" with its winglets, towered over the smaller aircraft in their midst.

Entering the Jet Base for the first time, I religiously followed the instructions that I had been given and reported to the security office. Everywhere I looked were red flying kangaroos emblazoned on doors, signs, and buildings. I had always been on the "blue team" across the way but now, here I was in Qantas heartland – the "red team".

Walking through the corridors of the Flight Training Centre, the walls were of towering glass. On the other side of these, the white flight simulators, with more red kangaroos, lurched on their hydraulic legs like futuristic Trojan horses. Sitting idle was the older Boeing 747 "Classic" simulator in which I was to attempt to demonstrate some degree of flying ability. This was almost the last hurdle. If I passed the simulator check, there was only a "medical" and police check to complete. If you received the call back after the simulator, you were virtually assured of a position. Fingers were crossed.

I was guided into a briefing room and given some power settings and aircraft attitudes to fly, which I promptly wrote on the back of my hand. The Check Captain etched out a plan for the exercise that included a Twin Locator approach and an Instrument Landing System, or ILS, precision approach. In between, there would be a range of climbs, descents, and turns onto specific headings.

By the time I strapped into the simulator my head was spinning and my heart was racing. A lot hinged on the next hour and as I scanned the flight deck, I was not overwhelmed with confidence. The Flight Engineer's panel sat on the side and was alien to me, although I wasn't expected to operate it for this session. The flight deck was larger than the 737, having four of everything, it gave the instrument panel and overhead switches a very busy and congested appearance.

The four thrust levers were of a far greater span than the familiar 737 and my stumpy fingers seemed to stretch to grip them. The engine power settings were in Engine Pressure Ratios, or EPRs, while I had been setting thrust using N1 values for the baby Boeing's CFM engines. And then there was the instrument panel – a maze of dials, while my last eight years had lulled me into a world of digital screens and easy-to-interpret map displays. Fortunately, I had continued to fly light aircraft, including old biplanes, and I hoped this would assist me with what lay ahead.

Soon enough, I rumbled down Sydney's runway 16 Right and eased the giant into the air. Its size made it feel incredibly stable and I wondered if the real aircraft felt so steady. Even so, my lack of recent flying was ringing alarm bells in my head. Rather than a smooth scan of the instruments, my eyeballs jumped erratically, searching for the relevant instrument before hunting back to another and making some adjustments.

The instructions kept coming thick and fast from the Check Captain. I forgot all about the settings scribbled on my hand and endeavoured to push and pull the 747 around the sky, fearful of overshooting an altitude or flying beyond some other limit. It wasn't pretty and I felt cumbersome. By the time the session had finished, I was sweating and dejected. The Check Captain shook my hand, saying very little more than, "We'll be in touch".

As I drove home, I cursed out loud at my ineptitude. I could fly better than that. Give me another shot. I'd blown it. What was I going to do? How do I tell Kirrily that I messed up?

It was the longest drive home that I can remember and as I walked into the house, the answering machine's small red light was blinking. At least it wouldn't be Qantas this quickly, I reassured myself. I hit the "Play" button.

"Hi, Owen. It's Robyn from Qantas. Can you call please me to arrange a time for your medical?"

Was I accepted? Well, not quite.

CHAPTER THREE
FROM THE GROUND UP.

Having been prodded and poked by the Medical Department and undoubtedly investigated by the Security Department to confirm that I wasn't a known felon, the waiting game began. This can be a torturous time for aspiring pilots as the timeframe can vary wildly. From an immediate phone call to being placed on an active "Hold File", a pilot can never be sure when that actual first day with an airline will arrive.

As I sat at home, waiting by the phone, Kirrily was in Cairns, where some senior crews and managers had gathered to farewell a long-serving and highly respected engineer. As a young First Officer, Kirrily was introduced to those gathered around the table, with her name striking an immediate note with one senior captain. "Kirrily Zupp? Zupp? Didn't we just give her husband a job?"

There was a stony silence and a sideward glance from an administration manager in the direction of the rather excited captain. Nothing was official yet and the information was not for distribution.

"Zupp. Yes, I'm sure that was the name. Ex-Ansett pilot. 737s, I think."

Realising the sensitive nature of the information, another pilot swiftly redirected the conversation and the awkwardness dissipated

– but it was too late. Beneath the table and out of sight, Kirrily was texting me on her phone. "I think you have the job! :-)"

It wasn't written in stone, but it was the most reassuring sign yet. The next thought that raced through my mind was as to which aircraft I would be assigned as a Second Officer. At the time, there was the Boeing 767, Boeing 747 "Classic" and the Boeing 747-400 fleets. My personal preference was the "400" for the destinations to which it flew, but I would be happy with any position I was offered. It wasn't long before the official call arrived and I was given a start date. My ground school training was to commence in four weeks and the aircraft was to be the Boeing 747-400. Perfect!

On my first day of training, the candidates all mingled in the coffee room and there were many familiar faces. With only two exceptions, the course was made up of ex-Ansett pilots like me.

We assembled in a room and were first briefed by a young Second Officer on the role and then welcomed to Qantas by the Training Manager. Then, after filling out forms and being measured for uniforms we were down to the business of learning about the engineering systems of the Boeing 747-400.

Overseeing our training was Steve Curtis. I'd known Steve in my life before airlines and it was no surprise that his prowess as an instructor was recognised and seized upon by the airline. Over the ensuing weeks, a combination of "chalk and talk" classroom lessons and digital presentations introduced us to the "Jumbo Jet". Most of us preferred the classroom to the droning voice of the computer's audio, still, there were exams to be passed and the information needed to be absorbed by whichever means it was delivered.

Even at this early stage, I was fascinated by the workings of the 747. I had often sat by a runway, waiting for my turn to take-off, when one would take-off or land in front of me. I had never given much thought to flying a 747 but the engineering was a wonder of the modern world. Its ability to lift a mammoth load and yet span the world at speed had always captured my attention. The complex system of high-lift devices that extended from the wings' leading and trailing edges defied belief. The massive undercarriage organised in groups of wheels, or "Bogies", and the distinctive hump of the upper deck had become longer and more graceful with each new model of the aircraft.

Applying the textbook theory to the aircraft was achieved through "fixed base" simulator sessions. In these lessons the simulator motion was inactive and the emphasis was on the switches and systems, the checklists and procedures. By replicating a failure, we could see how it would be indicated in the aircraft through the associated lights and warnings before performing the checklist in a slow methodical manner. There was no pressure to fly the simulator and at any point, the whole sequence could be stopped "in mid-air" and discussed. Step by step we came to know the 747 more intimately and at every turn, we were increasingly impressed.

Away from the simulator, the training centre also possessed a wooden mock-up of a 747 flight deck, complete with photographs of the instrumentation and panels attached. Here, office chairs could be slid into place and procedures rehearsed with "touch drills", reaching to where the actual switches were positioned. It was also a place where numerous calls could be practised to ensure that the words were correct and the flow seamless. This simple device was affectionately known as the "bamboo bomber" and even today, on any aircraft that I fly, I will spend some time in the "bomber" before a simulator check ride.

Away from the simulator and the bomber, there was a Dangerous Goods course and Security training which, in the wake of 9/11, also emphasised the importance of flight deck security and vigilance. Emergency Procedures training, or E.Ps, requires demonstrating proficiency in equipment and procedures in the case of an evacuation, ditching in the water, or other dire circumstances. Everything from flares to life jackets and raft management to escape slides and signalling with a mirror is covered in the syllabus. With many elements calling for a practical display of competency, we all geared up in white overalls with Qantas emblazoned across our backs. And when it came time for the "wet drill" in the pool, we donned life jackets to swim to the raft we had inflated, although the ideal scenario is to board the raft without getting wet.

E.Ps are conducted alongside cabin crew and revisited each year. They are the background skills that crew possess to assist passengers should an emergency take place as the cabin video discusses before each take-off. It is these very skills that make the difference when evacuating an aircraft in an event such as Sully's famous landing on the Hudson River.

The culmination of studying the procedures and aircraft systems is a series of examinations that inherently call for a pass of 80% or greater and in the case of some procedures, absolutely 100% word-perfect. As crew, it is an aspect of our profession of which the public is often unaware. Our skills are continually tested and refreshed, examined, and reviewed with a failure to meet the required standard calling for further training. The study never ceases throughout the career and the challenge is always there to perform. It is a love-hate aspect of the job for many but it's what keeps our passengers safe.

With the examinations completed, the trainees are paired up for their full-flight simulator training, with the pairings humorously referred to as "crash buddies". In my case, my crash buddy was Mike.

Mike and I had known each other as young freight pilots and even shared the same aircraft at one point. We had both been recruited by Ansett Australia as First Officers and we had both been made redundant in the collapse. It was a great pairing. Mike and I shared a certain sense of humour and he was a great "stick and rudder" manipulative pilot. With a common aviation history, we just clicked when it came to our training on the 747.

Flight simulator training can be demanding. Aside from the basic manipulation of take-off and landing, the training calls for the management of all imaginable emergencies. The required standard is uncompromising and at times the workload can be stressful, but I can honestly say that I genuinely enjoyed training on the 747 with Mike. We both had a multi-crew jet experience which gave us a head-start, with the most difficult aspect being to "unlearn" our Ansett terminology and replace it with the Qantas words.

Loss of cabin pressure, engine fires, hydraulic failures and more were thrown at us and throughout, the 747 was an incredibly stable platform. The aircraft made you look better than you probably were.

With the training complete, a date for our final check flight was set. The check ride was a standard and known quantity, so we had a fair idea of what to expect. While Mike and I studied alone, we still met up in the bomber to refine our procedures. When the day arrived, we were as ready as we were ever going to be. Sitting in the briefing room, the check captain had a wry grin as he surveyed our experience - we both had around 10,000 hours and significant jet time.

"You realise that I can vary the format of this check?" he asked.

Mike and I nodded in the affirmative but our thoughts were rather less positive.

Over the next four hours, we had all manner of "variations" presented for us to deal with. It was one of the toughest sessions we had both faced in a simulator. Fortunately, we managed to keep our heads above water and I'm sure that on occasions when the heat was on, we may have regressed to some of the words used by our old airline through an emergency procedure.

In the end, we sat in the debriefing room as the Check Captain silently wrote his review of our performance. We were well pleased when his only criticism was that some of our knowledge of company proce-dures was lacking and suggested that we read up on those. Without fanfare, he signed our forms, shook our hands, and sent us on our way.

We still had to undertake a training flight in the aircraft but for now, "Boeing 747" would soon be printed in my Flight Crew Licence.

CHAPTER FOUR
TAKING FLIGHT.

Intertwined with the ground school and flight simulator training was another component of becoming a Qantas 747 pilot – the familiarisation flight. It was a short flight, usually a domestic day trip, where the trainee could sit on the flight deck and witness the procedures at work. For my familiarisation, I was rostered as a "supernumerary" crew on a return flight to Cairns in far north Queensland, a trip of around three hours flight time each way.

It was a flight that I had made numerous times before, but this would be my first experience of the 747. As I fitted the wings, identity card and epaulettes to my shirt that morning, I looked at the lonely, single gold bar on the shoulder, recalling my single bar days as a trainee at Ansett a decade earlier. This was a new beginning in so many ways.

As I am prone to do, I ensured that I was at the Qantas briefing area early which left me standing there looking lost with nothing to do and in the crisp new uniform of a rookie. As I re-read the Notice Board for the fifteenth time, I sensed another pilot approaching and attempted to steal a glance at the name on his ID card. I was too slow.

"Owen Zupp?"

"Yes.", I answered, extending my hand.

"Dick Hodder. Your father, Phil, was my flying instructor in the 1960s!", he exclaimed.

I knew first-hand that my dad could be tough in the cockpit, so this introduction could still go either way.

"He was fantastic!"

I breathed again.

We were soon joined by Wayne, the First Officer for the day. We pored over the Notices to Airmen (NOTAMS), weather forecasts and charts before calculating an order for the amount of fuel we required. Throughout the process, there was a sense of familiarity as flying between Sydney and Cairns was my home turf. Setting out across the globe was their realm and I knew I would have a lot more to learn when we left Australian shores.

Stepping onto the flight deck for the first time, it seemed so much brighter. The simulator was lit with an artificial glow emanating from the screens that provided a visual representation. To walk onto the flight deck in natural light brought the flight deck alive. From the warmth to the touch of the centre pedestal to the small shadows cast by the switches, the reality was hitting home. This was indeed a real 747.

As the crew prepared for departure, I did my utmost to note down everything, saving any questions for when their workload was less. It was all coming together just as Mike and I had practised in the 'sim', further reinforcing the high level of standardisation that was expected by the airline.

With the doors closed and clearance obtained from Air Traffic Control, the tug began to push the giant aircraft back from the terminal. In due course, the engineer called, "Clear to start", through the headphones and Dick and Wayne brought the Rolls Royce engines to life. I scanned the gauges just as I had the 737, the numbers were different but the combination of fuel, spark, air and oil pressure were common to any engine.

As we taxied out to the runway, the ground seemed so very far away compared to the 737 and consequently, the sense of speed was entirely different. The nosewheel position was well behind the pilots' seats, so due allowance needed to be made on every turn to keep the aircraft central on the taxiway. And the main undercarriage was a long way back! Everything was on an impressive scale and the aircraft seemed to move with a blend of power and grace. When the time came to take off, the power was particularly noticeable.

Cleared for take-off, Dick brought the thrust levers up partially, allowing the engines to stabilise. He then pressed the "Take-Off, Go-Around", or TOGA, switch and the autothrottle drove the thrust levers forward to their required setting with Dick's right hand still on the levers.

With the engines so far from the flight deck compared to what I had been used to, the noise was a distant spooling up, followed by a gentle rumble as the 18 tyres gathered speed along the runway.

The acceleration was obvious with a gentle force pushing me back into the seat, but it was a calm release of energy. The airspeed was racing up the speed tape but there was no sense of urgency. The world slipped by in the peripheral vision at a polite distance. This was brute power going about its business with impeccable manners.

"V1" Wayne called the decision speed to reject the take-off or continue and Dick removed his hand from the thrust levers in response, further reinforcing the intent to continue should an engine fail.

"Rotate"

With two hands on the control column, Dick eased it towards him and the 747 responded by slowly raising its nose and setting course for the sky.

"Gear up"

The transition from rumbling earth-dweller into a flying machine was smooth and effortless. If there was any turbulence, it wasn't felt as the huge wings shrugged at such a minor interruption. Accelerating, the flaps were retracted to configure the 747 in its "clean" configuration, free to set course for the stratosphere, Cairns and the world of the Mach Number, where speed is expressed as a percentage of the speed of sound.

Settled in the cruise section of the flight, with the sun beaming into the flight deck, Dick began to relate his time as a Qantas Cadet Pilot and specifically, tales relating to my father, Phil. Dad had flown for Qantas in his own right as a First Officer in the days of the Super Constellation. The long absences of weeks at a time in the era of propeller-driven airliners was tough on families, particularly when my dad had spent years of his youth overseas during World War Two and the Korean War. In time, he tired of the life and resigned.

By the mid-1960s dad was tasked with training the cadet pilots for his former employer, Qantas. When young and fresh-faced, course number one arrived at the Illawarra Flying School at Bankstown, Dick Hodder was among their number.

Phil not only trained the next generation of airline pilots but kept them entertained with stories of flying Gloster Meteor fighter jets in combat and a dry sense of humour. Between lessons he would sometimes be called upon to tow banners announcing that "Waltham is a Good Watch", but it was the towing of targets that grabbed the attention of Dick and the other Qantas cadets.

The flying school also owned retired Mustang fighters that now wore civil schemes upon their flanks. Equipped with a winch and a small back seat for the winch operator, they would tow targets for the military to shoot at as Phil had done in his previous Air Force life. Sometimes the Mustangs were also flown in support of Army exercises and at other times, the Navy. On one pass of a warship, the gunners got a little too close for comfort, severing the target cable not too far from the Mustang's tail.

Each time the Mustang started its Merlin engine, Dick and the other cadets would rush to the fence and watch the famous fighter take to the sky. One afternoon, as they stood waiting, Phil opened the Mustang's throttle and roared down the runway. With its tail in the air and just about to lift off, the engine cut out and the take-off was abandoned. Phil brought the Mustang to a halt with very little airfield remaining. The students were aghast.

From their vantage point, the cadets could see the canopy slide back and Phil step down onto the wing before beginning the long walk back to the flight office. As he walked past, one cadet asked, "What happened Mr Zupp?" Without breaking stride, Phil replied, "I left my cushion in the office and I couldn't see over the nose of the aircraft." It was a reason the student pilots believed until later in the day when an engineer informed them that the engine had actually failed and shards of metal had been found within it. There were more stories and laughter shared as the 747 was navigated northward, with my regular interruptions to check on some aspect of the aircraft's operation.

Having being made redundant months earlier, the joy of being airborne again was an absolute pleasure. The familiar vista from the best office in the world, watching the earth slide by far below and the bubbling clouds growing as the morning warmed up. The hours passed quickly and soon the T/D symbology appeared at the top of the digital navigation display, or ND, to signal that the "Top of Descent" was approaching.

Dick and Wayne ran through their briefing, while I carefully noted down the format they used and the content that they covered. With the air traffic control clearance issued, the 747 was now upon the T/D and the four thrust levers were automatically commanded to slowly move back to idle. Except for some residual thrust, the jet was now effectively a 240-tonne glider. Again, everything about the aircraft felt stable and secure – it swept through the sky. Passing through a convective, cumulus cloud, it shrugged its shoulders when smaller craft would have been bounced around unceremoniously.

Like a massive magic carpet, it crossed the rugged terrain, the strip of sand and the crisp waters beneath to eventually align with the runway. Dick disengaged the autopilot and the audible warning "whooped' around the flight deck. The cross-hairs of the flight director sat steady in the middle as the aircraft slid down the ILS approach towards the runway.

In the last few hundred feet, we had been warned that the aircraft tended to fly up and "out of the slot" as a result of ground effect and it was a phenomenon we had witnessed in the simulator. Dick had flown the 747 too many times to be fooled and anticipated the trend with a subtle amount of forward pressure on the control column.

The radio altimeter counted down, calling out the height above the terrain below. In the last one hundred feet, Dick eased back on the column to raise the 747s nose to begin "flaring" the aeroplane. Descending through a cushion of air, the main wheels smoothly made contact with the runway, far removed from the flight deck where the speed brake lever rose from its armed position beside the now-closed thrust levers. Dick's right hand slid forward to grasp the reverse thrust levers to raise them partially to the "idle detent" which served to both provide adequate deceleration and a low noise level for the passengers in the cabin.

Exiting the runway, Dick and Wayne ran through their after-landing scans to "clean" the aircraft up in preparation for parking and disembarking the passengers. All the while I sat there quietly, impressed by the majestic way in which the 747 went about its business and wondering where my first trip would take me.

CHAPTER FIVE
SETTING COURSE.

I had always loved flying. As a young kid, I would convert every cardboard box into a Mustang fighter and relive dogfights of World War Two, even looking over my shoulder to "check my six". At other times I would sit on our roof with binoculars, watching the aircraft passing overhead. I was fortunate that in my years at Ansett I had kept flying light aircraft and even managed to retain my Flight Instructor Rating and train student pilots on occasions.

A particular highlight was when Kirrily and I were able to own our first aircraft – a de Havilland Tiger Moth. With a red fuselage and silver wings, it was a biplane from the days of old and had been the very type of aeroplane my dad had trained on decades before. With an "open cockpit" it required the pilots to wear helmets and goggles to keep the airflow at bay as they sat one behind the other in tandem. We had the luxury of an electric intercom to communicate, although the aircraft retained its original Gosport Tube, which was basically a rubber hose through which one pilot could yell to the other.

The backbone of Commonwealth pilot training during World War Two, our aircraft had served with the Royal Australian Air Force before being converted to cropduster. Its commercial career was short-lived, coming to grief in an accident in Western Australia where it remained in a darkened hangar for many years before being rescued. In a labour of love, we had engaged a team to restore the aircraft in a process that took years.

One of the great aspects of flying the Tiger Moth was the community that surrounded antique aeroplanes. Kirrily and I would travel to fly-ins, or participate in flypasts, each time meeting wonderful people with a common passion for aviation. One of those people was a Qantas 747 Captain, Sandy Howard.

Another captain once said to me that they suspected that Sandy ate bird seed as he flew so much. From Boeings to Tiger Moths, to restored Super Constellations and de Havilland Drovers, Sandy was a consummate aviator. He had known Kirrily's dad, Barrie, when he had flown the 747 for Qantas, although I came to become acquainted with Sandy through the Tiger Moth community. When it came to the Boeing 747, Sandy was a Senior Check and Training Captain who ultimately accumulated over 16,000 hours on the aircraft and countless more in the simulator. He had flown every variant of the type that Qantas had ever operated – the 100, 200, 300, 400, 400ER and the distinctive SP, or "Special Performance".

When Sandy called one morning, my thoughts firstly darted to flying the Tiger Moth but he was calling regarding another matter.

"I see that you're up for your PUIT trip."

PUIT was the abbreviation for "Pilot Under Initial Training" and the first flight "on the line" for a trainee was to be under the guidance of a training captain. I didn't have time to suspect what would come next.

"Would you like to come with me?"

I couldn't say "yes" fast enough. Not only would I be flying with someone that I knew, but Sandy would be a source of knowledge that I was keen to tap.

"Great. We are flying to Paris."

At that point, I almost fell over. Paris was a very "senior" trip meaning that you had to be checked out on the aircraft for quite some time before you would be at the front of the queue to bid for the French capital. In all likelihood, I would never again be senior enough to visit Paris, so this was a dream shot.

I excitedly told Kirrily to which she shared in my excitement with a high degree of envy I suspect as she was now flying the 767 and predominantly between Australian cities. I spent the next week reading everything that I could that related to Charles de Gaulle Airport in Paris and our enroute stop, Singapore's Changi Airport. And then there were the airways and airspace in between.

By the day of the flight, I was like a kid on his first day at school with a crisp new uniform and suitcase to match. Arriving early again, I printed out my sheet with the names of the crew which showed two other Second Officers. Sandy also arrived early and we waited for our flight folder to be delivered into the tray upon the desk of the briefing office. We took the opportunity to speak in person to the meteorological officers as a personal briefing can add so much to the printed charts and forecasts. The weather looked good with the standard chance of towering cumulus clouds and heavy rain in Singapore.

Our folder arrived at the same time as the rest of the crew, with each being allocated some part to read and note down relevant points. Sandy had offered the First Officer to fly the sector to Singapore, which he accepted, leaving Sandy the onwards flight to Paris. With the flying roles determined the crew gathered together to review the contents of the folder with an occasional comment among a constant flicking of paperwork before the crew came together to discuss what they had found. Through this process, an overall picture of the flight could be gained, including any navigation beacons or airports along the way which may not be available. Any weather or forecast turbulence to consider, or any issues with the serviceability of the aircraft.

All of these strands come together when considering the fuel order. It is often said that it "costs fuel to carry fuel". Explained simply, the heavier an aircraft is, the greater is the rate at which it burns fuel. Even through the course of a flight, fuel consumption decreases as the weight reduces. And of course, fuel costs money and airlines are a commercial venture.

Notwithstanding, airline crews will carry additional fuel to mitigate against a range of variables, from diverting around weather along the way to needing to have more than one attempt at landing at the destination because of weather or air traffic control issues. In the end, the crew will agree on how much fuel will be carried, ensuring that the figure at the very least meets the minimum amount legally required. With the planning process completed, Sandy led the way as we exited the building and boarded the airline's crew bus to deliver us to the aircraft.

Once at the aircraft, the Second Officers, or S/Os, sorted out their duties, just as the Captain and First Officer had done. In this case, it was to be "inside or outside", meaning one would undertake the external walkaround inspection while the other attended to the flight deck duties. I opted to remain on the flight deck in this instance as Steve Curtis had already demonstrated a very thorough external inspection.

Notebook in hand I shadowed the other S/O as he checked various certificates and documentation, programmed the ACARS, tested the High-Frequency radios and emergency oxygen masks. There was quite a list and it was all new to me. Fundamentally, the Second Officer is a support role to facilitate longer flight "tours of duty" and allowing the crew to gain sufficient rest. Additionally, and most critically, they can observe the overall operation from their seats behind the Captain and First Officer, providing timely input and assistance as needed. As a Captain, Sandy created an environment where any crew member was comfortable to raise concerns, which is a trademark of Australian flight decks across the airlines.

It is a role ideally suited to a pilot gaining their first multi-crew airline job, gaining valuable insights into the operation before moving into a front seat. Even so, it is a required right-of-passage for all recruits regardless of their experience. For a pilot like me who was recently unemployed, any seat was a privilege. And this seat was taking me to Paris!

CHAPTER SIX
A Brave New World.

In the wake of 9/11 came the bullet-proof flight deck door, thoroughly annexing the pilots from those whose care they were entrusted with. In times past, the crew could show their passengers the "office" but now it had been effectively reduced to a sealed vault. Even so, the sharp end of the 747 was a spacious workspace compared to those to which I was accustomed – it even had its own bathroom.

The Captain and First Officer sat in the front left and right seats respectively, separated by a wide centre console. This was home to the four thrust levers, and an array of radio selectors and panels to tune in navigation aids. From the left side, adjacent to the Captain's knee, rose the speedbrake lever to raise the panels from the wing's upper surface. The lever to the right extended and retracted the slats and flaps that called the wing's leading and trailing edges their home.

Directly behind the console was the "First Observer's Seat". Mounted on rails that could slide back and across to a fold-down table behind the First Officer, it was a seat that offered a panorama of the two pilots at work. To the left and behind the Captain was the "Second Observer's Seat" which was permanently fixed and offered a less ideal view of the operation but a reasonable view of the outside world through an adjacent window. For a long international sector, all four seats would be filled by pilots and with Paris the ultimate destination, that first afternoon was no exception.

Sandy Howard sat angled in his seat, his face towards the First Officer and the First Observer's seat. Through this simple act, he invited input from the crew and lowered the invisible barriers that a closed posture can raise. From there he managed the constant flow of information and interruptions that characterise a flight deck in the final hour before departure. From kindly cabin crew offering refreshments, to the arrival of maintenance documents and updated weather reports, the constant ebb and flow was a constant source of distraction that begs the crew to overlook some element of their preflight process.

Tasks were assigned throughout the crew and answers shared, all the while the hundreds of passengers made their way down the airport's umbilical cord and into the vast cabin of the 747. As the minutes counted down to departure, the tasks grew fewer and the focus finer. Calculations were made, confirming the speeds for take-off, including "V1", the "go/no-go" speed before which the take-off would be rejected and at which, or beyond, the take-off would be continued, even if an engine should fail.

These speeds, as well as the power settings for take-off, were calculated from a large five-centimetre-thick folder containing graphs for every runway in the network and offered variations in flap settings. The crew would each conduct their calculations independently before being cross-checked. Tailored flight paths in the event of an engine failure were also reviewed before the departure. These charts were in a map format and ensured terrain clearance in the case of decreased climb performance when the thrust was lost from an engine.

During a pause in the proceedings, the crew came together to discuss how they would fly the take-off and departure and the role each would play. With the First Officer flying the sector, he took the lead in the "briefing" after ensuring that he had the entire flight crew's attention. After considering any threats that may be lurking in the background, a full review of the departure was discussed, only pausing to allow Sandy to state and demonstrate his actions should he, as Captain, decide to reject the take-off on the runway. In closing, the First Officer called for input, suggestions and questions but the thorough briefing now had the crew on the same page and with a "shared mental model", as pilots are prone to say.

With the last passenger on board and the doors of the cargo holds closed, the remaining calculations of the aircraft's weight and balance were made. The details were compiled into a final "load sheet" and forwarded to the crew. The numbers contained were compared with those used in their calculations and various modifications made to the data within the 747's Flight Management Computer, or FMC. The take-off speeds were confirmed and any remaining paperwork was sent from the flight deck along with a warm farewell to the ground staff member who had been silently but eagerly waiting at the rear of the flight deck. As they disappeared through the door, the echo of a final call from the Cabin Manager reminded any remaining engineers or other ground staff that departure was imminent and that it was time to leave the aircraft.

The message on the central screen of the instrument panel warning the crew of an open door disappeared and prompted the remaining checklist items to be completed. The crew was ready and the radio call was made asking "Surface Movement Control" at Sydney Airport for clearance to push back and get underway. Without delay, clearance was given and the message was relayed to the engineer on the ground through the headsets plugged into the 747. The brakes were released and in a coordinated and oft-repeated act, the mighty giant was slowly pushed by a low and slow tug through a tow bar connected to the nose of the Boeing. Clear of the parking bay, the engineer cleared the pilots to start the four Rolls Royce engines and one by one, they slowly spooled up and came to life. Their vital signs conveyed through the instrument display confirmed that the 747 was now a living, breathing behemoth ready to take to the skies.

The brakes were again parked and the engineer cleared to disconnect their headset from the aircraft. Flaps were extended, more checklists completed and the engineer was set free with a final wave which they returned from the position beyond the wingtip. Another radio call, another clearance, brakes released and the aircraft slowly began to move under its own power.

The First Officer guided the 747 with a blend of thrust, brakes and direction through the steering wheel, or tiller, located by their knee on the wall of the flight deck.

Everyone's eyes were scanning outside, checking for wingtip clearance from obstacles, or a rogue ground vehicle that could threaten a collision.

As focused as I was, it was difficult to believe that I was there. Only a few months before my airline career had been in tatters and I was left wondering if it would ever recover. Sure, I had fallen to the bottom of the pecking order as a junior Second Officer in a new airline but I was still employed and had not had to relocate overseas like so many of my good friends. And here I was on a 747 bound for Paris.

Cleared to cross Runway 07/25 at Sydney, I scanned outside once more and everything seemed so far below compared to my previous aircraft, the "Baby Boeing" 737. At this height, speed was also deceptive. The journey out to the runway seemed slow and majestic, yet on checking the ground speed the 747 was moving at more than 20 knots. Everything was on a scale that I had never imagined and now as part of the crew with a seat on the flight deck, the reality was sinking in.

Soon after, I was sinking into my seat as the take-off roll began. With the nosewheel far below the flight deck, the runway beneath the wheels was a mere rumble compared to the loud rattle in the 737. The pause between the "Go- NoGo" speed of V1, to the "Rotate" speed of VR was far greater than I had ever experienced on smaller jets. And while it is a function of physics, it more subtly conveyed that the 747 would take to the sky on its terms – with grace and not haste. After all, it is a Queen.

The airport terminals and then the city of Sydney fell away beneath the wings. Guided into a left turn to set course, the 747 swept all before it like a magic carpet that shrugged off any hint of turbulence. It had no time for annoying bubbles of rising air or passing showers and maintained its composure with its eye on the greater purpose.

Climbing away over the Blue Mountains to the west of Sydney, the shadows below were lengthening. The First Officer engaged the autopilot and Sandy took over control and immediately invited me to climb into the front seat that his co-pilot had vacated. I eagerly manoeuvered my way into the seat, careful not to rest my hand somewhere dumb and push a switch – or worse.

Seated, I pushed the switches on the side of the seat to drive the electric motors. With each short, high-pitched hum the seat moved fore or aft, up or down, until I felt comfortable with the outlook ahead and my position in relation to the controls.

"Happy?" Sandy asked.

"Yep." How could I not be happy?

"Handing Over." He followed up without delay. Sandy knew of my aviation journey and sensed the significance of this moment for me.

"Taking Over." I realised that he had just put the flight path of this magnificent aircraft beneath my hands, albeit through the autopilot. My eyes scanned the instrument panel and the world outside with a sense of childlike excitement.

"Are you going to fly it?" Sandy asked in the voice of a heartfelt aviator and a smile to match.

I looked back with an even larger grin and then set my gaze ahead once more as my right thumb reached for the autopilot disconnect button on the control column.

"Disconnecting," I announced.

CHAPTER SEVEN
THE FIRST DANCE.

M y thumb silently squeezed the disconnect button, sending the warning system momentarily into its fit of sirens and flashing lights, before a second squeeze restored the calm. My eyes fell into the scan in which they had been trained, eking out data from the relevant instrument before moving to the next, processing the results and applying the required piloting response before commencing the scan again. With the sun setting outside and the horizon clear to be seen, the scan became a relaxed cycle of my eyes venturing to the world outside and then back into the instrument panel.

My first impression of this legendary aircraft was its feeling of inherent stability. Its sheer mass bullied the air out of its way and any input from me was met with the smoothest return from the aircraft. It wanted to remain exactly where the pilot put it, and if disturbed, would return to that place with minimal effort and little more than an aerodynamic sigh for the interruption. Passing over a waypoint that signalled a change in course I applied the smallest input and the 747 wheeled about the sky like a yacht on the breeze with the perfect amount of sail.

And when it came time to cease climbing and settle in for the cruise, the nose was lowered just a few degrees, the speed settled and the thrust relaxed. It was with some reluctance that I engaged the autopilot once more and relinquished the control inputs back to the aircraft and its systems.

A roster had been drawn up and the first of the pilots to take a break made their way to their respective crew rest facilities. I was in no hurry to leave the front seat and the red folder that I'd brought on board had a series of questions that Sandy needed to ask me and "sign off" before we returned from Paris. There was plenty of time for that.

I handed control of the aircraft back to Sandy, content to keep the flight log and manage the radio communications now that the autopilot had replaced my hands. I watched the last rays of sunlight fan out from the horizon as central Australia slid beneath our wings. The world below was already in darkness and the isolated towns were pinpoints of light spread thinly across the black canvas of the outback. Ultimately, the sunlight slipped from sight, replaced by the stars that grew increasingly brighter as the night prevailed.

The sound of subsonic airflow whispered as it slipped around the flight deck's windows and I momentarily craned my neck to look back at the wing tip with its steady green navigation light and brightly blinking strobe. Was someone down there craning their neck skyward to gaze upon the light show overhead?

From my earliest days, I had loved flying at night. There was less chatter on the airwaves and generally smoother conditions. A sense of serenity could be found that daylight did not seem to offer in the same way. And if the moon were out, clouds would come alive, allowing me to steer among the towering cumulus with grace, while being reminded of how small I was in the greater scheme of things.

For now, my eyes and thoughts returned to the instrument panel as we approached another waypoint and then passed over it. I took the clipboard down from its place atop the instrument panel and clicked my pen into life. I logged the details of time, speed over the ground, or groundspeed, fuel used and fuel that remained. I calculated our time over the next waypoint, changed the frequency on our radio panel and transmitted our position.

Stowing the clipboard once again, Sandy and I began to chat about the 747, our destination Singapore and the subsequent passage to Paris. He had seemed to have respected my silence of the past hour, perhaps he perceived that I was deep in thought and appreciating the opportunity to fly once again.

As Sandy, like me, was an aviation enthusiast beyond the confines of the flight deck he undoubtedly appreciated the uncertainty that had befallen me over the past six months. Although, I had been fortunate to still take to the skies for an hour here and there in an old biplane, where the wind whistled in the wires and only a leather helmet and goggles separated me from the elements. Beautiful simplicity.

Now, I had returned to the expansive flight deck with its air conditioning and a vast range of technology. There was no chance of a map being blown out of the cockpit, or spits of oil flicking back into my face as the biplane offered. No, this was another world, a descendant of that wood, rag, and tube airframe but so very different. I mused how the Wright Brothers' first flight was over a smaller distance than the vast wingspan of this mighty Boeing 747. A distance that conveniently formed a potential question from the red folder through which Sandy began to browse.

The time passed at pace as it always does when everything is new and begs investigation. Even so, I had to take my time away from the flight deck to ensure the level of rest that flight crew are required to have on long-haul operations. When I vacated the seat, it was necessary to inform the pilot now filling that seat of the state of the flight. Where we were, who we were communicating with, the status of the aircraft and the distribution of its fuel load and how the flight was progressing compared to the original flight plan. They were all details that the crew share whenever a changeover takes place.

With the briefing completed, I made my way back from the flight deck, between sleeping business class passengers, to the rear of the upper deck of the 747. I poked my head around the bulkhead where a lone flight attendant sat in the galley, reading a magazine to stay awake. We chatted for a few minutes before I stepped back and opened the cupboard door that was the entrance to the aft flight crew rest.

It was a small, concealed place where a lone reclined seat lay waiting for me to make my bed and drift to sleep. I slipped off my boots and changed my uniform shirt for something more comfortable and less prone to creasing. I sat back down and contemplated sleep in a state of drowsiness and conflicting excitement. Switching the light off, I plunged the cavity into darkness and laid back, clipping the seat belt loosely about my waist.

I considered the air sweeping past at nearly the speed of sound only a matter of centimetres from my head, separated by aluminium, cabin lining and insulation. Down through my seat, the floor and the passengers and cargo below the frigid air fell away to the warm waters of the Timor Sea, perhaps the island shores of Indonesia by now. My mind bounced around some basic mathematics of time, speed, and distance but I only fell more into a reluctant trance.

What was the name of that next expanse of water? The Java Sea? Yes, the Java Sea.

And then sleep folded my mind's map and put it away.

CHAPTER EIGHT
SLIPPING IN SINGAPORE.

Most of my knowledge of Singapore was gleaned from history books, with a focus on the Japanese advance from the north in World War Two that ultimately ended with the surrender of the allied forces. I had read of the troops subsequent incarceration at Changi Prison Camp and forced labour on the Thai-Burma railway. I knew a gentleman who had survived this ordeal.

Singapore's Changi Aiport was close to the site of the wartime prison, although the glow of lights breaking through the cloud cover ahead spoke of a very different place. As the 747 was progressively readied for landing, tall buildings with red beacons on their rooftops provided a very different vista to the dark days of the war. The blinking strobes of an aircraft ahead and the radio transmissions of multiple aircraft behind gave the feeling of nocturnal birds coming home to roost after a long night aloft. We passed over the runway's end and soon the rumble of the airframe signalled that the wheels had returned to earth and the reverse thrust had been deployed to an idle setting.

Exiting the bright lights of the runway edges, the call came to "Follow the greens". On cue, a thread of green lights glowed from the centre of the taxiway, guiding us to our parking bay with tailored precision. The usual task of navigating a foreign labyrinth of taxiways in the darkness was incredibly simplified in a way that I had never previously witnessed.

I was equally amazed as we drove to the hotel when I was informed that the towering trees that lined the motorway were fake and could be removed – along with the traffic lights and signage. The purpose of this potential redesign was for the motorway to serve as a runway if needed.

Our hotel was in the heart of Singapore and its grand foyer caught me a little off guard. International airline crews spent more time in ports overseas and the hotels at which Qantas crews rested were first class as I was to soon learn. I was also introduced to the "envelope". To cover meals when in port, each crew member was given an envelope with a generous amount of cash in the local currency. Reading the expression on my face, one of the crew explained that it was calculated on dining in the second tier restaurant within the hotel. I began to mentally calculate how my "allowances" may ultimately fund our next holiday as I was prone to a light breakfast, a reasonable lunch and dinner. It was on the matter of dinner that I would gain yet another introduction at "Fattys" the following evening.

Arriving in my room, I was impressed by the grand scale. As was my habit, I unpacked my bag and proceeded to iron my uniform shirt, regardless of the late hour and despite there being nearly 48 hours until I departed. I always slept better if I knew I was ready to go if plans changed. It had been a long night and the added excitement of this brave new world added to my fatigue.

The next day I set about exploring Singapore with a folded map in my hand and a backpack over my shoulder. I had been instructed not to J-walk, cross against the lights, or chew gum as all were frowned upon and fined by the authorities in the very organised city of Singapore. While the rest of the crew had gone in search of well-priced cameras and computer parts, I was content to venture on a walk of discovery.

Stepping from the foyer, I was immediately blinded as my sunglasses fogged over on contact with the steamy tropical air. It was a clash between the chill of air conditioning and the humidity of ambient air that was to become commonplace. I walked through the famed Raffles Hotel, the home of the Singapore Sling cocktail. With its grand white façade topped with a flagpole, courtyard and turning circle, it reeked of colonial times. Inside, oversized paper fans hung from the roof, moving too and fro in unison. It was here at Raffles that my father stayed in his days with Qantas in the 1950s and I couldn't help but wonder if he had walked down these very corridors.

From Raffles, I caught a cab to Sentosa Island to visit Fort Siloso for a whirlwind tour. The fort was one of the original gun batteries from World War Two that Great Britain had established as part of "Fortress Singapore". As history records, the fortress fell. The guns were now silent and manned by mannequins of soldiers, frozen in time. I pondered the contrast between being a tourist and being one of those desperately loading those cannons so long ago. Where I stood, they stood a lifetime before. How many never returned home?

The restaurant known as "Fattys" was a Qantas institution. The rumour was that Fatty's family had smuggled food to Australian prisoners in Changi Prison during World War Two and ever since, crews transiting Singapore had returned the favour with constant custom and generous tips. Ironically, the owners, Fatty and Skinny were both very slight in frame but cooked the finest Asian food that I had ever tasted.

We sat around one of the numerous garden tables outside and joined forces with one of the southbound crews. Many tales were told at Fattys – some tall, some true, some both and some neither. Good company was never in short supply I discovered. I had never been much of a beer drinker but I was introduced to a brew by the name of Tsingtao that night. Originating from a brewery started by Germans who settled in China a century before, the beer was light and refreshing in the heat of a Singapore evening and was one of the creative ways that Fatty used to calculate the bill for the evening. He would cast his eye over the table, the number of empty plates and Tsingtao bottles and arrive at a total. It was always fair, well received and had little basis in reality. The bill was never challenged and to the contrary, crews added something extra. It was all part of the tradition.

The next morning I met Sandy for breakfast before retreating to my room and studying the route to Paris and other pertinent procedures. After a few hours in the books, I set them aside and readied for sleep before the inevitable call summoned me to depart.

As I waited for slumber to seep in, the significance of the fort was

not lost on me and I considered how many places of historical importance this new chapter in my aviation career would permit me to visit.
The collapse of Ansett had left me unemployed, destined to start over
again but somehow it had also re-directed my life. I felt a real sense that
opportunities were waiting for me. One flight deck door had closed
but another had opened. And this was the door of the Boeing 747 – the
Queen of the Skies.

CHAPTER NINE
Bound For Europe.

My eyes opened slowly and the small red LED at the base of the television was the only light in the blacked-out room. I felt blindly for my bedside table, but it seemed to have shifted - that's strange. With my left hand I reached out across the bed for Kirrily – but she wasn't there! I went from a doze to being startled in a microsecond. Where is she? Where the hell am I?

I fumbled for the lamp, but it had also changed location and ever so slowly, the realisation dawned upon me. I wasn't at home. I had returned to the nomadic life of a pilot and the need to orientate myself each time that I woke up in a different city.

My next fear was that I'd overslept. The alarm was still thirty minutes from heralding its message, but I decided to kick back the covers and get ready anyway. That would leave time for a relaxing cup of tea and a final review of the charts before heading downstairs and departing.

It was April of 2002 and the coalition's bombing campaign in Afghanistan was in full swing, preventing civilian aircraft from transiting the airspace. Further complicating the issue, sections of Iraqi airspace were also no-fly zones, so a modified route tonight would take us over the Persian Gulf, adding at least half an hour of flight time and burning more fuel. We chatted about the closure of our usual route over Afghanistan and the implications of this as the bus made its way to Changi Airport.

I had been warned not to lose sight of the crew at Changi as the corridors leading to the crew's briefing room were a maze and more than one pilot had been lost there over the years. Sandy laid out the flight plan and I was aghast at the ream of green and white striped computer paper which was longer than I was tall. There were a dozen pages of navigation log with pages at either end, detailing fuel plans, decision points to divert and enroute winds among other information. When I was flying from Sydney to Melbourne, the log had featured a dozen waypoints along the way – this plan featured more like a hundred it seemed. Against the name of each waypoint was printed the planned flight level, track, distance, forecast wind, groundspeed, time interval and planned fuel remaining. Small dots beside each data field left space to enter actual figures and times.

One task for the Second Officer on departure was to note the time and progressively add the intervals to calculate the estimated time of arrival at the destination. An error in the addition could leave the flight plan looking like a piece of graffiti with crossed out numbers and new figures scribbled over the top. The standing joke was that the mathematical error always seemed to be on page one – leaving twelve pages of corrections to be completed by a very embarrassed S/O.

The crew performed the ritual of reading each page of information relating to the flight before discussing it in terms of the fuel load that would be required. The flight time would be more than twelve hours with the weather over Europe forecast to be fine. Even so, the crew agreed upon a figure that allowed an arrival into Paris with adequate fuel to divert to another airport if needed. Fortunately, Europe was awash with relatively close airports that could accommodate a Boeing 747.

Once the fuel order was phoned through, I made my way to the aircraft keeping the crew close by for fear of being lost in the maze. As we readied the aircraft for departure, another task for the S/O was to check that the full range of charts was on board to cover the entire route and all available airports along the way. The charts were carried in two large leather flight bags, to ensure two copies of everything. It was a laborious task but critical in that an emergency diversion would not be helped by a missing arrival chart to some distant airfield.

With the last passengers and bags safely on board, the final load sheet was handed to Sandy, outlining exactly what we were carrying in terms of people, payload, and fuel. There is a saying that an aircraft is ready to depart when the weight of the paperwork equals the weight of the aircraft, and I was learning that it echoed the truth for a long international sector.

Soon Singapore was a memory and the black abyss of the Bay of Bengal slipped silently beneath us. Soon we were "handed off" the clear VHF radio communication frequency of Singapore to call Mumbai on a very scratchy HF frequency to gain clearance to transit Indian airspace. It took all my concentration and strained my hearing to decipher what the air traffic controller was asking for as I struggled to report our position. Fortunately, Sandy was prompting me and finally, I had relayed the information that he needed – or so I thought. The controller then transmitted a single word.

"Raj"

I was confused. "Raj"? I was aware of the British Raj as the governing body of colonial India, but that arrangement had ceased in 1947 with India gaining independence.

"Say again"? I asked.

"Raj"

I looked across at Sandy who wore a wry grin, amused at my lack of understanding

"Qantas 17. Qantas 17. Say again"?

"Raj"

"Thanks. Qantas 17" Sandy intervened before solving the mystery. Still smiling, Sandy explained, "He was saying 'Rog' - as in short for Roger."

It was as simple as Roger, meaning message received. I smiled too and fortunately, the dim light of the flight deck hid my embarrassment.

Settled in for the long haul to Paris, Sandy and I paired off and we discussed some of the many questions across a range of topics contained within my red training folder. Rather than an interrogation, Sandy availed his years of 747 experience to give the stark facts, living, breathing detail. I noted each point down, fascinated by the story that accompanied each of them.

From India we crossed the Arabian Sea to Saudi Arabia, remaining to the south of Iraq's restricted airspace, although by this time I was in the bunk counting miles and drifting off to sleep to the now-familiar sound of the near-supersonic air slipping past the airframe near my head. It was the deep slumber that comes with any form of training and study, although it was abruptly interrupted when the door to the crew rest was flung open and light from the rear galley poured in.

Confused, I could see an equally confused gentleman trying to get his bearings as he ducked under the door frame into my sleeping quarters.

"Can I help you"? I queried, rising onto one elbow, still restrained by the seat belt.

"Is this the toilet"?

"I hope not. This is where I sleep"!

Without another word, he stumbled back, closed the door, and engaged the flight attendant in conversation in a rather loud voice. The spell was broken, and I was wide awake once again. I pulled on my uniform shirt and felt a pin prick. It was the backing of my father's "Qantas Empire Airways" pilot wings which I had resolved to carry with me on my first flight with Qantas. Dad had passed a decade before, but I thought he should make the trip with me in some form. I made my way back to the flight deck and sat in one of the observer seats, waiting for Sandy to wake up and return.

I chatted with the crew and noted our position. I had drawn the route in my Collins World Atlas and moved a small sticky note in the shape of an arrow further along the line. In addition to the navigation charts, the atlas offered a better representation of the planet beneath me, rather than solely focusing on airways and airports. I was fascinated by the concept of crossing half the planet in a single night and pondered how a boy from a small fibro house in the western suburbs of Sydney had the world this far beneath his feet. All the while, the 747 strode past another border and another country at nearly 500 knots.

Beyond the Mediterranean and another rest break, we closed in on Charles de Gaulle Airport in Paris as the sun climbed above the horizon. Again, the crew gathered for Sandy's briefing that detailed the various aspects of our arrival. As forecast, the weather was fine, and we had sufficient fuel to reach several European airports if the need arose.

As we approached the top of descent, the cabin crew came to the flight deck and cleared the plates and cups that had borne our breakfast and paused to take in the view out ahead. Perhaps a glimpse of the Eiffel Tower – no – still too far away.

No sooner had the engines retarded to idle and the 747 had gracefully lowered its nose to descend than French air traffic control began to issue us with vectors, or headings to steer. Left and right the Queen swept about the sky, guided by Sandy's steady hand. Whether we were being vectored around other aircraft climbing and descending, we couldn't be sure because the controller had resorted to giving instructions to other aircraft in French!

English is the official language of aviation, but this controller had lapsed into his native tongue when speaking with French pilots. The problem was that all pilots gain a "mental model" of where other aircraft are based on hearing these instructions. I could vaguely make out some numbers and "descendre" but otherwise, I couldn't grasp a single word.

I peered out towards the northwest and could make out central Paris and maybe, just maybe, I could see the Eiffel Tower peeking up from the skyline. However, the focus was on the flight path as Charles De Gaulle Airport became increasingly evident out the window.

In perfect conditions, we touched down and rolled to a speed suitable to exit the runway. I ran my finger along an airport chart, tracking the taxi instructions to the terminal which thankfully were in English. Parked and silent, the Queen of the Skies had reached her destination safely again.

Sandy turned towards the crew and asked for any feedback regarding the arrival. A short debrief after each flight is a critical tool in maintaining standards and encouraging comments is a healthy means of improving. The common thread related to the vectoring and the use of the local language but otherwise the arrival into Paris was uneventful.

I unlocked the flight deck door and began to pack the charts away when I noticed a placard above each of the pilots' side windows. Despite having been in the seat for hours during the night, only now did they grab my attention. They indicated the aircraft's "name." While this 747 was officially registered VH-OJO, Qantas also named their aircraft after an Australian township.

This aircraft was the "City of Toowoomba" – my dad's hometown. I felt for his wings in my pocket and sat quietly for a moment. Perhaps he had travelled with me after all.

CHAPTER TEN
PARIS. THE CITY OF LOVE.

I t was a sensory overload.

Part of my passion for flying stemmed from a passion for exploring. Whether it was abandoned mines near the Turon River or the swamp near our local football fields, I always wanted to go a little further and see a little more. Aviation had taken me far beyond the football fields and I greedily consumed every new sight, sound, and smell that I could.

This curiosity even extended to the bus ride from the airport to the hotel that generally found the crew taking a well-deserved nap after a long night in the skies. By contrast, I took in the architecture, the cars, people – even the street signs and number plates. It was all new, exciting, and different to me. I was tired but my mind was buzzing.

Arriving at the hotel I explored my room with the same enthusiasm. It was small, much smaller than the room in Singapore but neat and modern. Unpack, iron shirt, hang clothes. The wardrobe was tiny, such that my clothes hung on an angle to close the door. Mini fridge, mini bar, stationery set…map! I opened out the map and orientated myself. The sun outside my window allowed me to roughly calculate North and align the map in the correct sense.

I laid out my pre-written list of tourist objectives and marked them off on the map, forming a plan of attack. The Arc de Triomphe was some distance away and represented a sound starting point to work from. There was a "Metro" station not far from the hotel, so my strategy was set. I loaded up my backpack with a bottle of water and a jacket and set out on my journey, map in hand. Leaving the hotel, I noticed that the corridor was peppered with "Do Not Disturb" signs on door handles, hung there by the crew. I was far too excited to sleep – this was Paris!

The Arc de Triomphe towered above me, far more impressive than any image in a book could ever convey. A project initiated by Emperor Napoleon; he would only pass beneath the completed arch in death. Here victors and tyrants alike had entered Paris, the centrepiece of the city, encircled by a plaza and, in turn, a roadway, with streets radiating out like spokes from a hub. Consequently, many of the nearby buildings were located on triangular parcels of land.

At the apex of one triangle, I came across a small Parisian café that could have featured as the backdrop for a movie. Its tall glass windows were framed in carved wood and lace curtains were tied back to show waitresses moving left and right, serving the clientele. Outside, small round tables were covered in red and white checked tablecloths, their chairs also of carved wood with plush fabric cushions.

With the sun shining, I opted for the fresh air and sat down. Perusing the menu, I found that it was entirely in French - not surprisingly in retrospect. As a schoolboy, I had been, without doubt, the worst student of the French language any teacher had ever been tasked with educating. Memories of trying to bend my broad Australian accent to the demure tones of Francais came flooding back. I could recall the words for "please", "thank you" and the numbers up to ten. There was only one thing to do, pick a meal by number and point at the menu.

Soon a young lass made her way to my table, offering the broadest of smiles. Without a word, she placed a jug of water and a clean glass in front of me and I suspected that her mastery of English paralleled my expertise with French.

I raised the menu and pointed to whatever food had been labelled as number three. My mouth was dry, and my lips slowly formed the words.

"Trois, s'l vous plait." Even I could tell that I had just butchered the French language.

"Are you Australian"? She fired back with an equally broad drawl. "Yes"!

"Wow! I'm from Geelong"! she said with the high pitch of an excited tourist.

My Parisian experience came crashing down, albeit to the warmth of an Aussie welcome.

After some pate, cheese and I suspect sea urchins, I began my trek to the Eiffel Tower. I crossed a bridge spanning the Seine River and gazed at the waters that had filled countless passages of literature as the tower loomed larger. On reaching the landmark, I stood beneath it and gazed up at the spire, its superstructure a web of intertwined steel.

It was through the air beneath these arches that United States Army Air Force pilot, Captain Bill Overstreet chased a German Bf109 fighter in 1944. While the Eiffel Tower reaches beyond 1,000 feet, the first floor sits only 180 feet above the ground and spanned 400 feet at the base with the arches reducing the clearance even further. It would've been a wild ride and no doubt the adrenalin was flowing for both the hunter and the hunted.

I bought my ticket and climbed the 674 steps to the second floor, the limit of public access. I wandered about taking in the view from each vantage point but by far my favourite was the view down the vast green expanse of the Champ de Mars (Field of Mars). Nearly a kilometre long, the public park ran from the base of the tower to the historic military college, Ecole Militaire, founded in 1750.

As I walked towards the college, I could see myriad contrails overhead as I had never seen before. The incredible amount of air traffic over Europe was crisscrossing in every direction and filling the sky with their markers. At ground level, I reached the walls of the college which still bore the scars of bullets striking their flanks in World War Two.

A left turn and some distance further and I entered the grounds of Les Invalides. Built in the 17th century for aged and disabled soldiers, it was now a massive military museum with artefacts of all types dating back to the Napoleonic era. Not only were there numerous weapons, armour, and insignia on display but the mortal remains of Napoleon now rest in a massive sarcophagus.

The hours disappeared as I wandered the corridors of Les Invalides until fatigue began to creep into my bones. I was still a distance from the hotel, but I resolved to walk along the banks of the Seine and drink in every drop of history despite my eyes begging me to close them.

I entered my room and slipped my own "Do Not Disturb" sign over the door handle. I showered quickly to wake a little more and sat on my bed, phone card in hand, ready to call Kirrily as it was now morning in Sydney.

I woke fourteen hours later with the phone card still beside me. I never made the call.

CHAPTER ELEVEN
HEADING HOME.

I woke up tired and hungry – a common state for international air crew. There were several notes under my door from the night before inviting me to dinner which I had overlooked in my exercise-induced coma. I still had a few items on my travel agenda, such as the site of The Bastille, and the famed Notre Dame Cathedral, however, there was also work to be done, so it was a whirlwind tour that day.

A side of airline operations not commonly appreciated is the ongoing commitment by flight crew to study and standards. A few times each year pilots are called to be checked in the simulator, in addition to ground school days encompassing topics such as emergency procedures, security protocols, and the carriage of dangerous goods. Rigorous medical standards must also be maintained and proven to retain the privileges of an Airline Transport Pilot Licence, or ATPL. During a career, promotions and the conversion to different aircraft types called for months of further training, with periodic checks of progress. So, despite the majesty of Paris calling from beyond my window, a good many hours were spent in the books, further educating myself in the ways of my new airline and new aircraft.

Qantas operated the Boeing 747-400, powered by four Rolls Royce engines, although the airline was soon to receive "Extended Range", or ER, variants of the prolific airliner. The ER would be fundamentally the same airframe but carry additional fuel, allowing it to fly further. It would also carry engines produced by General Electric, or GE. The introduction of the 747-400ER would not call for a full endorsement, but a course in the "differences" between the GE and RR powered aircraft. For the moment, my hands were full studying the established Rolls Royce 747-400.

The more that I read the books, the more I continued to be fascinated by the aircraft's engineering. That it could fly so far and so fast had changed the world of air travel, but for me, the "high lift devices" had always captured my attention – and the attention of nearly every passenger that I ever met.

The "high lift devices" were those metallic panels that extended from the front "leading" edge of the wing and the rear "trailing" edge as an aircraft prepared for take-off or approached to land. The 747 asked its wings to lift almost four hundred tonnes and travel close to the speed of sound, while still achieving flight at speeds slow enough to take-off on a reasonable length of runway and land on the same. It achieved this by changing its wings' shape and curvature using these devices to suit the task it was being asked to perform. Modern airliners all share this feature, but the intricacy, sequencing and engineering of the Boeing 747 was always something to behold – and studied.

All too soon it was time to farewell Paris, not knowing if I would ever be senior enough to fly there again as crew. With bags packed and my uniform on, the ritual began once again. The crew met in the foyer, discussed the flight ahead on the bus to the airport before disembarking and making our way through the terminal at Charles de Gaulle. I noticed a dull "thump" could be heard at regular intervals. It seemed to emanate from below, in the bowels of the airport.

"Thump"! Again, it grabbed my attention as I placed my suitcase on the scales to be weighed and checked in.

"What's that noise"? I asked the agent that tagged my bag.

"Explosions."

"Pardon"?

"They are blowing up unattended bags that were found in the terminal."

It was a poignant reminder that the terrorist attacks of 9/11 had occurred only seven months earlier and that the world was still very much on edge. Even more recently, Richard Reid had boarded a flight at this very airport, Charles de Gaulle, and attempted to detonate a shoe bomb on a flight bound for Miami.

With the military coalition's response to 9/11 still closing Afghanistan's airspace, we were again routed south to Singapore via the Persian Gulf. The journey home was relaxed with Sandy educating me rather than interrogating me. I began to feel more at home in my surroundings in the 747 and had time to drink in the diverse scenery by day and the limitless display of stars and planets by night.

The sunrises and sunsets were something very special. I had always treasured the privilege of seeing a day being born and put to rest and the way those first and last rays tinged clouds and painted the sky. Now the horizon was taking on different forms - jagged ranges, snow-capped mountains, water masses of different depths, colours, and surfaces. As a blue-blooded aviator, Sandy also valued these moments and an unofficial pause in conversation would take place. Perhaps a word or two of admiration for what lay beyond the window, or a reference to some relevant history or fact that was passing beneath our wings. Otherwise, these were cherished, quiet moments.

These were sights that I would not have witnessed had a cruel twist of fate cast my career in a new direction. And yet that twist of fate was rapidly losing its bite as if I had been put at a disadvantage in my career but given a rare opportunity in the broader scope of life. Perhaps I should share this? Perhaps I should write about this world above our planet? It was a thought for another sunrise, for now, my compass was set for Singapore and then home.

When the 747 finally eased to a halt at its parking bay at Sydney Airport, the fuel was cut off from the engines and the red flashing beacon signalled the aircraft was now at rest. Procedures were followed and checklists completed, the flight deck was tidied, and goodbyes were exchanged as duty-free shopping and Customs queues would often separate a crew.

Sandy and I had waited behind and he drew my red training folder from beside his seat. It was all but completed and only the flight time for this final sector needed to be entered and signed off. He flicked through the pages one more time to check that nothing had been missed. It was Sandy – nothing had been missed.

Content that all that needed to be said had been said over the preceding week, he shook my hand and welcomed me to the ranks of Qantas pilots with an open invitation to contact him should I ever have any questions. I knew that I would have many.

We parted company and I was driven home by a car provided by the airline for pilots after long tours of duty. In the back seat, my eyes grew heavy, and I looked at the red folder jutting forth from my flight bag. Signed, sealed and yet to be delivered. The final step was to submit my completed training file and officially receive my new epaulettes which would now carry two gold bars.

I was back at the bottom of the tree as a somewhat older than average Second Officer with a new airline, a new aircraft and a new network that reached around the planet. I let my eyelids win the battle – a new chapter of my career was just beginning. Life was good.

PART TWO
A New Beginning.

CHAPTER TWELVE
A DIFFERENT WORLD.

Freshly qualified to operate the Boeing 747-400, there was no doubt that the world of aviation was now a vastly different place to that of my childhood.

My parents had both served in the Royal Australian Air Force, my father as a fighter pilot and my mother as a wartime radar operator – a "Hush Hush Girl." They told tales from their childhood of barnstorming pilots landing on local farms and taking folks for their first flight in frail machines with open cockpits. Airfields were far more developed by my childhood, but the ability to interact with aeroplanes and pilots was still commonplace.

Airfields were littered with new private aircraft, while older classic aeroplanes fired up their engines with puffs of smoke, and old warbirds, now in civilian garb, roared skyward to tow targets for the military. There was all manner of wings to climb upon and instrument panels to gaze at through hands cupped on Perspex windows.

As long as I paid due respect to taxiways and people's property, there were no limitations upon a budding young aviator like me. Free to wander and explore, query and question. And those who called the airport their home could not encourage the next generation enough, hoisting them into seats and on occasions taking them for that prized goal - a lap of the airfield! A small camera with twelve valued frames of film was standard equipment and the week's wait for them to be developed was too long to bear. The entire experience of a visit to the airport was about as good as it could get for a keen youngster.

When it came to my turn to occupy the flight deck, a constant stream of passengers would visit our office, with a fortunate few invited to stay for the landing. There were few rigorous security protocols, just common sense, and good manners. Aviation was to be shared, just as it had been throughout my childhood.

And then the events of 11th September 2001 took place and forever changed our world. The flight deck visits were replaced by bulletproof doors and the harsh reality of the 21st Century was thrust upon the industry.

The enhanced security measures were inevitable and necessary, not only to deter those who would attack an aircraft but to provide some degree of confidence in the industry for those who chose to fly. For me, it drew a major line across my aviation career in recalling the days before the attacks and those days that followed 9/11.

My transition to international airline operations following the attacks exposed me to the reality of the new world at close quarters. My first flight to Paris in 2002 had been only a few months after Richard Reid had boarded an aircraft at the same French airport, planning to take down an aircraft with an explosive shoe, prompting the removal of shoes at all airport security checkpoints. Over the ensuing years, I was caught up operationally in other threats against airlines – two in London and one in New York.

Putting on my uniform in the Gloucester Millennium Hotel in London on Valentine's Day, 2003 was anything but a sweetheart arrangement. The BBC had been broadcasting that a potential threat existed against airliners operating from Heathrow Airport in the form of surface-to-air-missiles, or SAMs. Relatively cheap, shoulder-mounted, and portable, the authorities had recognised SAMs as a genuine threat since one had been fired at an airliner taking off from Mombasa, Kenya the preceding November. But something had increased the level of concern in London.

When our crew bus entered Heathrow Airport, the difference in setting was immediately evident. Huge military and police vehicles lined the way and Kevlar-vested troops bearing automatic weapons took control of every corner. The military presence only intensified as we entered the terminal building, and the security checkpoints were slowed to a crawl with personal and baggage checks being conducted in incredible detail – no stone would be left unturned by the authorities or the airlines. I had no fear for our safety throughout the experience, but the scene would have been considered a work of fiction only a few years earlier.

The close of 2003 in New York echoed the tension of London earlier that year. I had been fortunate to be called to operate to the "Big Apple" and had enjoyed a wonderful few days based out of our hotel at the heart of Times Square. We were to fly out on New Year's Eve and miss the massive celebration that Times Square traditionally offered as a new year dawned but there was no mistaking the buzz as the city readied for its night of nights. However, the buzz of helicopters overhead hinted at something more sinister.

The FBI reported that they had four times the normal number of personnel on hand and Times Square was central to the plan. A 'No Fly Zone" was established around the city and a Congressman on the House Select Committee on Homeland Security was urging people not to travel to Times Square.

We departed early that evening for the airport to escape any chance of traffic delays and arrived at the airport where an extremely high-security presence was on hand. Again, Kevlar vests, automatic weapons and earpieces were the state of dress for security forces cruising the terminal. Airside, the airport seemed to be in relative darkness as airliners were moving about with their logo lights extinguished, plunging their fins into darkness rather than illuminating their airline's insignia. It made for interesting compliance with taxi instructions when we were told to follow a "United," or "Continental" Boeing 757 as all we could see was the dull glow of their wingtip-mounted navigation lights. Just as in London months before, I felt secure in the procedures in place but was struck by the scenes that I witnessed.

August 2006 found me in London once more and Heathrow under a heavy veil of security. A plot had just been foiled in which terrorists had planned to bring down a number of aircraft over the Atlantic. The terrorists had proposed bringing on board innocent-looking fluids in containers that they would mix and ignite mid-flight. Fortunately, the plan had been under surveillance for some time when the authorities shut it down.

Even so, Heathrow was again the scene of a military presence and enhanced security measures. In addition to removing shoes and belts, the carriage of liquids and gels was now restricted in a measure that was enforced worldwide.

Being proximal to genuine threats against aviation reminded me how far we had fallen since the innocent days of wandering around airfields unescorted. While part of me longed for those days, I realised that they were gone and that airlines and authorities around the world had a duty of care to their staff and customers that they took very seriously. Security training for crews was introduced and tightened procedures on the ground and in the air were necessary steps to ensure safety in a new environment.

It was a backdrop that I knew would lie below the surface of all operations as I travelled the world, aware that vigilance would be paramount, whether flying or spending time in port. It was not the career that I had foreseen as a starry-eyed boy, peering through windows into empty cockpits. But then again, how many careers ever truly went to plan?

CHAPTER THIRTEEN
GOING THE DISTANCE.

From when the Boeing 747 first entered commercial service in 1970 it began to make the world a smaller place. Spanning oceans and placing international travel within the affordable reach of many more passengers, the 747 changed the face of civil aviation. The aircraft would grow in its own right through a range of variants, each building upon the knowledge gained from the one before.

The 747-400 appeared to have met all the required goals when the aircraft was able to transit the 7,000 miles of Pacific Ocean to join Australia's east coast with the United States' west. Still, the quest for even greater range saw the genesis of the Boeing 747-400ER – Extended Range. Only six "ERs" were built in the passenger configuration, and all were delivered to Qantas. Aside from arriving overhead existing destinations with more fuel in the tanks, it opened up new routes such as direct services between Los Angeles and Melbourne and Brisbane and Dallas.

The ER achieved this by an additional fuel tank located in the fuselage, just forward of the existing centre wing tank found in the standard 747-400s. The "auxiliary" tank held just over 12,000 litres, or 9,700kg, of fuel and gave the ER even longer legs. The total fuel capacity across eight tanks was a staggering 227,700 litres and weighing in at 182,800 kg.

VH-OEF "Sydney" was the first ER to enter service in November 2002 and I was fortunate to crew the aircraft to London only a couple of weeks later, complete with that new car smell. However, it would be four years later that the fuel capacity of a 747-400ER would be particularly relevant for me.

It was approaching Christmas in 2006 and the Victorian landscape was in the grip of savage bushfires with smoke filling the air in the east above the Victorian Alps. So severe were the fires that the smoke was causing issues as far away as Melbourne Airport, from where we were scheduled to depart for Los Angeles (LAX).

The aircraft was VH-OEI "Ceduna", and the captain was Bill Anderson, a gentleman of the highest order. The trip meant that the crew wouldn't be home for Christmas, but we would find a way to celebrate, nevertheless. With a full load, the ER could take to the sky at a weight of just over 412 tonnes and the long haul to Los Angeles was a sector that called for this. The take-off and initial climb were normal but very soon thereafter the outboard engine on the right wing, "Number Four", began generating a significant vibration.

All four pilots were on the flight deck at the time and checklists were methodically read from the Quick Reference Handbook, or "QRH" as Bill managed the aircraft and considered the available options. Without delay, it was decided to shut down the offending engine, which was no issue for the 747, although we were no longer bound for Los Angeles.

With the engine secured and the aircraft safe in level flight, the next issue was that we were still more than 100 tonnes above our maximum landing weight of 289,000 kg. We had to jettison around 125,000 litres of jet fuel! To add to the situation, we were currently overflying the Victorian bushfires, a fact not lost on the air traffic controller when we requested clearance to dump the fuel. In reality, there was no issue as fuel being jettisoned dissipates well before it ever reaches the ground.

With no urgency to land, Sydney was our main maintenance base and afforded our passengers the greatest chance of being rescheduled quickly onto another service to LAX. In addition to managing the aircraft and preparing for our arrival in Sydney, our cabin crew needed to be briefed and our passengers kept informed and reassured, particularly as the process of jettisoning fuel would be visible from the cabin.

We made our way east to a position off the NSW coast and began the procedure which saw the fuel stream from nozzles mounted inboard of the wingtip and along the trailing edge of the wing. After around two hours aloft, we began our descent into Sydney where we landed without event, taxied in, and parked the magnificent jet. Bill debriefed the entire crew about what had happened before we all went our separate ways.

For some, it meant that Christmas would now be spent with family. For me, Kirrily and the kids were in Queensland, and I was relegated to a standby roster. A few days later, I was in Melbourne once again and bound for Los Angeles. The second attempt went without a hitch, this time the aircraft was the newest ER and the final Boeing 747 that Qantas ever received. The aircraft was VH-OEJ, "Wunala".

The shutdown of the number four engine was the only inflight technical issue that I had experienced on the 747. Day after day, night after night, its four engines hummed rhythmically as the miles slipped by, many thousands of feet below. Pacific crossings usually entailed a late afternoon departure that slipped quickly into the night before a sunrise beamed into the flight deck as the US west coast approached.

On those long nights of darkness, there was constant monitoring of the aircraft, checking of weather forecasts and periodic hypothetical planning to cater for where we would go if something occurred enroute, but fortunately, that never happened. In between, there were hours to converse with the other pilot, or quietly contemplate.

A moonlit night was a blessing, illuminating towering cumulus clouds like massive billowing pillars in the sky. Some near the equator were like thin arms of coral reaching 40,000 feet, while others banded together to form massive walls of weather. I wondered how much water was within those tumultuous storms and how that water would be liquid gold to the drought-stricken farmers at home.

I would often spot the lone light of a vessel far below, ploughing through the waves in darkness and contemplated the difference in the ways we traversed the Pacific Ocean and the lives we led. I considered Sir Charles Kingsford Smith and his crew in 1928, flying the first trans-Pacific crossing in their three-engined, fabric-covered "Southern Cross".

Down low, amongst the weather and with little to navigate by, they departed Oakland and hopped their tiny aircraft across the vast expanse, stopping at Hawaii and Fiji before making landfall at Brisbane on the Australian east coast. Flying at around 80mph, the one leg from Hawaii to Fiji alone had the crew aloft for just under 35 hours – we could transit the entire ocean in around 13.

Additionally, they were confronted by weather they could not see in the darkness whereas I could scan the weather radar 100 miles ahead and gently divert the jet twenty miles clear of any storms and comfortably watch the amazing light show in wonder from a safe distance and in air-conditioned comfort. Aviation had come so very far in the span of a single lifetime.

All the while the four engines of the 747 spoke softly and without complaint. We fed them fuel and they gave us speed and altitude – it was a fair exchange. Another minute, another eight miles closer to Los Angeles.

CHAPTER FOURTEEN
THE SKY ABOVE.

Flying above the world's magnificent landscapes, it was easy to assume that all the planet's majesty was terrestrial. However, there were many intriguing sights to be seen in the sky above, particularly by night.

Perched at altitude, high above the earth, the vista was not contaminated by city lights or obscured by layers of haze. The air was clear and crisp, offering up a sea of stars that coated the sky. The cross-section of the Milky Way lived up to its name as 100 billion stars merged into a glittering viscous mass. Planets were more obvious, and Venus shone just that much brighter before dawn when viewed from altitude.

Yet not all celestial bodies I gazed upon were heavenly in nature. Man-made satellites consistently carved their path, one after the other, leaving long trails of green or orange as they burned up attempting to return home to our atmosphere. Not the mere flashes we glimpse from the ground, but dramatic slow swathes of colour lasting for seconds.

And then there was the International Space Station (ISS), launched in 1998 and orbiting 400km above our humble Boeing 747. Brighter than any star, the ISS would sweep by, covering 8 kilometres every second, or more than 27,000 km/h.

In my bag, I carried a star chart, an oversized circular slide rule with which I could identify the stars and planets that surrounded me. I could identify the various constellations and in my mind's eye draw the creatures they were said to portray – a lion, a scorpion. It was a bare, black canvas with billions of pin holes letting through shards of light. And one evening that light was brilliant.

While Honolulu lay only a matter of miles away, the passengers on board the 747 were blissfully unaware, curled up beneath their blankets in the darkened cabin. The cabin crew chatted in hushed tones behind the galley's heavy curtains, planning their shopping strategy when they arrived in San Francisco in a few hours.

On the flight deck, the tone was also hushed so as not to disturb the resting crew at the compartment's rear. The aircraft continued to track faultlessly along the magenta line on the instrument flight display as the 'Top of Descent' indicator and San Francisco edged ever closer down the screen. I called up the latest weather reports through the aircraft's onboard system and shared them with my fellow pilot. It was set to be a beautiful day, but we ran through all our available options and fuel status to ensure that all the bases were covered.

The first rays of the sun had not yet crept above the horizon, but a portion of the upper atmosphere was revealing the first traces of the new day. A light, faint haze met the curved shadow of the earth's outline in an arc that spanned the horizon from left to right. The day was encroaching on the stratosphere, but not yet on the earth below.

The first indication that something special was taking place was not visual. It was the chatter between American crews transiting the busy route between the mainland and Hawaii. "Can you see that?" "What is it?" and "Is someone starting World War Three?" The exchanges piqued my interest but did not indicate the location or nature of the commotion. Then there was a hint. "There. On the horizon. Down low. It's brilliant!"

I leaned forward in my seat and peered into the darkness below. Nothing. Resting my arms on the top of the instrument panel, I cupped my eyes with my hands to keep the glow of the instrument panel to a minimum. Then I saw it. A tiny, bright intense light, like the tip of a white-hot arc welder. Almost stationary, it was growing larger, ever so slightly. In a matter of seconds, it grew from a needle point to a distinct flame, growing both in mass and momentum at a rate that was difficult to comprehend.

"What is it?" the other pilot echoed my thoughts, equally astounded. Still, it grew every second to a brighter and more impressive light, darting skyward. There was no perspective available to gauge distance or offer an idea of its size, just an ever-increasing intensity. Then someone identified the UFO that was captivating every crew aloft that night. "It's a launch out of Vandenberg."

A rocket launch from the United States Air Force base on the west coast. Now everything made sense. It was hundreds of miles away, but so powerful that it was seen by every aircraft in the flight levels and as it climbed it seemed to grow in speed as its trajectory could now be viewed in profile. Up through the darkness and onwards towards the illuminated upper atmosphere, the rocket would reach the daylight before the night's end for any of the citizens below. In a spectacular display of sheer energy, the projectile closed in on the arc between night and day, dark and light. One almost expected it to tear through some barrier between dawn like ripping fabric. And then it did.

Just as its furious flightpath penetrated the arc.

Wooomf!

A flash of light lit up the night for an instant before a mammoth expanding ring of vapour exploded across the sky. Like those TV documentaries that show the final burst of light across the galaxy from a dying star, such was the scope of this amazing sight. It was the rocket jettisoning a stage of its cylindrical being to leave the 'sharp end' to continue its journey into 'earth orbit'. Bound for space and relieved of much of its load, the remaining portion seemed to accelerate ever-faster and ever-higher. I craned my neck to look skyward and follow the lone beacon as it roared away and finally faded from my mere mortal sight.

Wow!

It had departed as quickly as it had emerged. All that remained was the ring across the horizon which was now merging with the moisture to develop into a cloud system of its own, as an atmospheric calling card. Its passage had been silent, but its impact was immense. Meanwhile, the four engines of the 747 continued to hum hypnotically, the cabin crew chatted in the galley and the passengers slept, blissfully unaware.

I continued to look toward where I had last seen the rocket's efflux, but it was now just another patch of darkened sky with innumerable pinholes of light. As John Gillespie Magee described so brilliantly in his famous poem, "High Flight," it had, …" slipped the surly bonds of Earth."

CHAPTER FIFTEEN
LONDON CALLING.

The Qantas network for the 747 was diverse, spanning several continents and oceans. From Europe to the United States, Johannesburg to Asia and multiple ports of call in between, it was the best possible way I could ever have imagined seeing the world. The number of days in different ports varied, as did the time away from home. Certain destinations were favoured in the winter months and others in the summer. The choice was broad and the longer that I was in the airline, the more pilots joined the fleet behind me, meaning that I had an ever-increasing chance of getting the trips that I bid for. Those bids often led me to London.

My wife Kirrily had been a pilot on the 747 when she first joined Qantas and, in an era before children, I had travelled with her as a passenger to London when she was a member of the operating crew. Such trips gave me an early insight into long-haul flying as it was a time when I could visit the cockpit and view Kirrily and the other pilots at work. At the time, I did not imagine that I would ever be operating a 747 into London as I was very content plying my trade in a 737 across Australia.

The city itself fuelled my passion for history and the summer flying season of air shows was something to behold for an aviation enthusiast. Beyond the city limits the "green and pleasant lands" offered small roadside taverns dating back centuries and charming "bed and breakfast" accommodation. It was no wonder that Kirrily and I spent our honeymoon based out of London, after a stopover in New York. Now it was my turn to crew the 747 to one of our favourite cities.

The Qantas flight to London was known as the "Kangaroo Route" and dated back to 1935 when the airline, then known as "Qantas Empire Airways", would fly to Singapore and hand its passengers onto the British "Imperial Airways" aircraft in exchange for its southbound passengers. The journey would involve more than twenty refuelling stops along the way and the fare was a King's ransom. Still, the service provided a speedier link between the Mother Country and her colony in the Antipodes than any ship could provide. Now, a trip that once took two weeks could be achieved in less than 24 hours of flight time, straddling the earth with a single stop in Singapore. Although other routes linked Australia to London, the route via Singapore that carried the flight number of "QF1" remained known as the Kangaroo Route.

Late in 2002, with the coalition in total control of the air, the flight from Singapore to London was able to resume its normal route through Afghanistan's airspace, saving the time and miles that the Persian Gulf transit had added. It was on this more direct sector from Singapore that I first crossed the India-Pakistan border. The two nations were not the best of friends, and this seemed to flow onto their air traffic control system. On occasions, we had to manage our radio frequency transfer and keep a keen ear out for other traffic as the respective air traffic controllers seemed to have failed to communicate with each other in the standard fashion of "handing off" an aircraft to another controller. However, it was the view of the border by night that took my breath away.

Dividing the darkness, a solid line of lights separated the two nations, from the Arabian Sea to the Himalayas. Along that line, barbed wire and troops stood guard beneath lights so bright that they can be seen from space. I pondered the cost of maintaining such a vivid line in the sand and the levels of poverty in those same two nations as I stared down at the otherwise darkened landscape.

Beyond Pakistan, the passage through Afghanistan's airspace was via a corridor with very defined procedures and controlled by the coalition. Ground-based navigation aids in Afghanistan were non-existent after years of neglect, but as modern airliners carried autonomous navigation systems that offered high levels of precision, this was not an issue. Airliners flew a pre-programmed air route with the final airways clearance to transit being granted by a military airborne controller.

The initial clearance to transit the corridor was required before departure and conditions of entry including aircraft "squawking" a transponder code to be identified on radar and to have the aircraft's tail illuminated with the logo light, in addition to other external lighting. There were also requirements relating to the altitude and speeds to be flown. If all the conditions were met, the airborne controller we contacted by VHF radio well before the boundary of the airspace to seek clearance.

The controller would be on board an "Airborne Early Warning and Control" (AWACs) aircraft. Essentially, the aircraft was a highly modified Boeing 707 or 767 with a massive rotating disc mounted above its fuselage. This disc could interrogate all aircraft in the area and coordinate their safe passage. Operating under callsigns such as "Boss Man," we would gain our clearance from a friendly American voice and report our progress to the AWACs controller until leaving the corridor and entering Turkmenistan. The corridor would be replaced by traditional air traffic control in the years that followed by Kabul Area Control Centre, a ground-based unit and operated by civilian contractors.

The subsequent route carried us through Eastern Europe where the scratchy transmissions of HF radio had given way to the clearer tones of VHF, although the deep, broad accents of the controllers still made comprehension difficult. The long hours and numerous nations were behind us as we reached the final, high workload hour of the flight. In the winter months, the arrival at London's Heathrow airport was made in darkness.

As we approached Western Europe my interest was always peaked. The nations that had filled my textbooks and imagination as a youth began to slip under the nose of the 747. Germany, the Netherlands, Belgium, and France seemed as though you could throw a net over them and yet it was difficult to imagine cramming all their combined history into a galaxy, let alone such a small patch of earth. Ahead, a dark strip appeared and was no doubt the English Channel where Armadas had once sailed, and furious battles aloft had seen Spitfires and Messerschmitts clash in the Battle of Britain.

As I considered the glow of our flight panel and its colourful, informative displays, and enjoyed the warmth of the flight deck and hot coffee, I thought of young men who never knew such luxury. These were the crews of the allied air forces in World War Two. Freezing in their deafening multi-engined bombers, the sight of the Thames would have meant so very much more. It was the first hint that they might have just defied the odds and survived the night. Even so, their aircraft may have been limping home, battle-damaged after the crossed beams had caught them and the anti-aircraft fire brutalised them. Some of the crew may have been bandaged and bleeding, praying for the moment when the wheels again touched down on the soil of Mother England between the blazing paths of burning oil that lit the runway's edge.

They may well have not seen the Thames or the blacked-out city of London, hidden beneath a low cover of English stratus. Feeling their way back home, edging down foot by foot until their base, or any suitable airfield offered them salvation. There was no cabin crew preparing omelettes on a hot plate for these young men and I felt a pang of guilt and indebtedness as I recalled the comfortable wonder of my flight.

Mere boys at the helm of lumbering machines launched into the darkened war-torn skies with a poor chance of ever making it back. Those in Bomber Command had a loss rate of over 40 per cent and more than 50,000 young men never came home.

Dawn was still a little way off as the River Thames appeared, as we weaved through the densely lit city of London and lined up to land at Heathrow. As the air traffic controller unhurriedly spoke to a multitude of aeroplanes, we extended the flaps, lowered the wheels and readied to land. The wonders of automation steered the course and allowed the crew the brain-space to manage the giant Boeing through its final, busy moments of flight before the autopilot was disengaged and the 747 and its precious passengers rejoined the earth. The Kangaroo Route had been completed once more.

Flying the return leg of the Kangaroo Route would sometimes be varied, transiting via Bangkok, although Singapore remained the port most associated with the history of the route. As a Second Officer, one of the less desirable trips involved a "double shuttle". Rather than heading home directly from London, a short "slip" in Bangkok saw the S/O return to London for a second time for another couple of days in the United Kingdom before finally completing the journey home, to Sydney.

The trip wasn't the most popular as it lasted thirteen days and involved joining a different crew on nearly every sector. It was much shorter than the trips that lasted for weeks in my father's era flying the propeller-driven Super Constellation for Qantas, but with a young family, I still missed the time away from them. The other less than desirable side effect was the jet lag associated with multiple east-west sectors in a short space of time. All long-haul crew experience some degree of staring at the walls from midnight to 3 am, but the double shuttle magnified the intensity. I'm sure that there were nights I flew past my "body clock" over Kabul, heading in the opposite direction.

Still, whether via Singapore or Bangkok, there was also an element of joy to be heading home. Planning the uplift of fuel on the sector to Asia often generated interesting discussions. Simply put, carrying fuel makes an aircraft heavier and a heavier aircraft burns more fuel. Consequently, it costs fuel to carry additional fuel and as fuel constitutes a major expense of operations, calculating a fuel order was never as simple as filling the tanks to full.

Compounding the decision were several factors, particularly the presence of adverse weather in the afternoon in Bangkok or Singapore, just when we were scheduled to arrive. The storms and low clouds were common but not necessarily forecast, although experience dictated extra fuel should be uplifted to cover the possibility. It was not a legal requirement, but it was a prudent decision in the interests of safety.

Additionally, despite the cost of carrying the fuel, the cost of having to divert could be far greater. A diversion could see the crew reaching the limit of their "tour of duty", preventing them from completing the flight. Rather than arriving in Bangkok and holding until the weather cleared, a diversion to Chiang Mai would see the need to accommodate hundreds of passengers at a port not normally supported by the airline's ground crew. These were all considerations as the crew sat in the briefing room, discussing the amount of fuel to be carried. This was part of the planning in flying any sector, international or domestic.

Regardless of the route, the time away and the wonderful cities that were visited, home always remained the favourite destination.

The Qantas Boeing 747-400 Simulator.

Sydney Harbour during a farewell "joy flight". (Image: Kirrily Zupp)

Owen and Kirrily Zupp at the Canberra farewell flight. (Image: Tony Lucas).

Phillip Zupp's QEA "wings" and other mementos.

A final farewell wave from the crew.
Top to Bottom of stairs.
Captains Ewen Cameron and Sharelle Quinn.
Second Officer Owen Zupp and First Officer Quin Ledden.
Captains Owen Weaver and Greg Fitzgerald.

The inside view of Sydney's water cannon goodbye.

The crew in flight, creating the kangaroo "Sky Art"

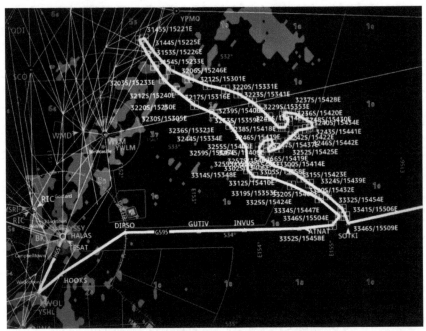

The kangaroo "Sky Art" and its 75 waypoints.

Final flight cakes before departing Los Angeles for the Mojave Air and Space Port.

Captain Ewen Cameron signing the log to accept "Wunala" for its final journey.

Mojave Air and Space Port from above.

Runway Ahead. Captain Ewen Cameron approaching touchdown at Mojave.

Disembarking "Wunala" at Mojave.

Captain Sharelle Quinn seated in the engine cowling of "Wunala" following the final flight.

Four Qantas Boeing 747-400ER aircraft at rest at Mojave.

The original "Wunala" VH-OJB. Fading away in the desert sun of Mojave.

The last look back.

CHAPTER SIXTEEN
HIGHER GROUND.

While the Kangaroo Route was the traditional air link between Australia and England, it was not the only route that Qantas flew between the two nations. The passage was also achieved via Hong Kong and transiting the higher latitudes of the Northern Hemisphere.

My only overseas travel as a youth was an air force cadet exchange to Hong Kong where my memories included being given a flight in a Tiger Moth biplane. We flew a series of aerobatic manoeuvres including a wonderful loop and I recall the airflow rushing past my bare face as we approached to land. There was no such sensation on the flight deck of the 747 when I returned to Hong Kong twenty years later, nor was the dramatic arrival to Kai Tak Airport via the "chequerboard". The new airport was built on reclaimed land on the island of Chek Lap Kok, around 25km from Kai Tak.

A bustling city, it generally came to life mid-morning and worked well into the night. I would take the opportunity to run in the pre-dawn hours when the city was silent except for the occasional garbage truck. It was not the only city where this was my habit but the contrast between the buzz of the city only a few hours later was significant. Between walking to the fish markets and climbing "The Peak" later in the day, it made my jogging efforts almost unnecessary on what was a short transit.

When the time came to depart in the evening, the planning was more complex than normal. An additional consideration was the cold temperatures that we would encounter flying so far north, particularly in the winter months. Of prime concern was the temperature of the fuel and to avoid it freezing. The 747 had a quoted limitation for the fuel of minus 47 degrees Celsius but under certain circumstances, and based on the grade of fuel, that temperature would be changed to minus 40 degrees. Accordingly, our flight plan before departure would include a table with predicted fuel temperatures along the route. The aircraft also possessed a display indicating the fuel temperature in flight which turned amber on dropping to minus 37 degrees Celsius and triggered an advisory message of "FUEL TEMP LOW" to alert the crew. I only saw the message twice, once between Hong Kong and London and the other was a long way south and at the other end of the planet.

If this message occurred, the crew had a couple of straightforward options to raise the fuel temperature. The first was to accelerate, allowing the increased friction of the air upon the wing to generate heat and warm the wing and therefore the fuel. It is this same mechanism that warms the aircraft and fuel on any flight.

At 36,000 feet the actual outside air temperature is in the realm of minus 56 degrees Celsius, however, flying at Mach 0.8 warms the aircraft skin to around minus 29 degrees. This raised temperature resulting from the friction of high-speed flight is known as the Total Air Temperature, or TAT, in aviation jargon. The cautionary note is that the increased thrust to fly faster means that the engines burn more fuel, so calculations needed to be made to assess the impact on the fuel remaining at the destination. Any such acceleration was only for a certain period, so the impact was not necessarily great, but it was a consideration.

The second fuel warming tactic was to descend into warmer air, as the atmosphere cools at roughly two degrees per thousand feet. Descending four thousand feet could potentially raise the temperature by eight degrees. Like accelerating, flight at lower levels also equated to burning fuel at a greater rate and this needed to be assessed. The fuel temperature tables we were supplied preflight were yet another valuable tool in calculating our fuel uplift in advance and could determine our cruising altitudes and speeds in the planning phase.

An aspect of the sector between London and Hong Kong that was shared with its counterpart over Afghanistan was the presence of high terrain – very high terrain. Commercial aviation has maintained its level of safety by mitigating against possible emergencies well in advance through planning and training, even if those emergencies were extremely rare. One such situation is the loss of "pressurisation", the system that provides oxygen and warm conditioned air to the cabin while the air outside is less friendly to humans. Before each flight, the cabin crew brief the passengers about the loss of pressurisation and how the masks will drop from the ceiling to provide oxygen. On the flight deck, the crew will also fit oxygen masks as their first action before they descend quickly to a level where the ambient air provided breathable levels of oxygen.

Australia is a relatively flat country, so an emergency descent to 10,000 feet where the air is oxygen-rich doesn't present an issue. However, the proposed route across China featured terrain far higher than the Australian landscape. In places, the minimum altitude to which an aircraft can safely descend is over 18,000 feet and while this offered some reprieve, it was not adequate, and an "Escape Route" strategy existed.

The escape route consisted of multiple branches veering off the planned route at different points and offering guidance to lower ground and ultimately an alternate airport. The escape route was preprogrammed by the pilots into the Flight Management Computer (FMC) so that in the event of a depressurisation, the plan could be executed with the push of a few buttons and a minimum of time. To my knowledge, no Qantas aircraft has ever used the strategy, but crews have always trained for the event and had their FMCs programmed and at the ready.

Even in the summer months, most of the spectacular terrain was invisible beneath us, wrapped in the shroud of nightfall. Despite this, the arrival into London by day on a crisp, clear morning would offer up a special treat. Inevitably, a delay would be required, and we would be instructed to enter the holding pattern at Lambourne. It was peak hour, and we would not be the only aircraft carving out a racetrack pattern to the north of London.

From our vantage point, we could see other aircraft sweeping into turns, stacked high, a thousand feet vertically separating one from the other. The sun would glint off the polished finish of the American Airlines 757 and fins of all colours and all nations would slice through the sky above and below us. Like a well-choreographed swirling dance, each passed Lambourne, turned left and started timing their outbound leg, progressively being stepped down as the lowest aircraft in the stack was granted clearance to approach and land. It was like a personal air show of civil airliners.

From Lambourne, we would head southwest past Wembley Stadium with London city further out to our left-hand side before joining final for Runway 27 at Heathrow. Runway 27 Right was furthest from the terminal, and it could take a further half-hour, if not longer, to cross Runway 27 Left and finally park at our assigned bay. Even so, it was always worth the wait in an English summer.

On the ground, I would cover countless miles in a day walking past Buckingham Palace, through Hyde Park and beyond. The Tower of London, Lord's Cricket Ground, Westminster Abbey, and museum after museum. And then there were the air shows.

A train ride to Old Warden would see me visit the Shuttleworth collection which included frail wood and fabric aircraft from flight's earliest days flying in the twilight to the accompaniment of classical music and popping corks. The smell of castor oil would fill the air as the ancient engines played to their own tune. The roar of classic fighters and bombers at the wartime base at Duxford was something entirely different. Deafening, fast and yet graceful, the warbirds would bank and roll before joining up for massive formation fly pasts.

It was appropriate that on one trip I was able to co-ordinate a Hong Kong to London sector to launch my first book, "Down to Earth", at Duxford. The book detailed the wartime experiences of Squadron Leader Kenneth McGlashan AFC, a Battle of Britain veteran who had been shot down over Dunkirk among many other adventures. Kirrily and our young daughter, Ruby, had made the trip with me and as I sat in a tent with famed wartime pilots and my little family I was once again struck by the amazing turn that my life had taken. When the time came to leave London and return to Hong Kong after Duxford, it was fitting that the departure held something special in store.

As the 747 climbed away from Heathrow, inbound traffic caused the controller to steer us away from the standard flight path and limit our climb. The consequence was that we sped across the southeast of England at a relatively low altitude. Initially, the White Cliffs of Dover passed beneath our wing as we climbed up through the skies over the English Channel and Dunkirk on the French Coast. I had just retraced Squadron Leader McGlashan's flight path on the fateful day that he was shot down and now the very stretch of beach where he abandoned his ditched aircraft lay before me. My spine tingled.

A couple of hours later as daylight was fading and we made our way east, we were flying over modern-day Poland in a region that had once been part of the Kingdom of Prussia. It was from there that my ancestors had made the journey to Hamburg and then the treacherous sea voyage to Australia in 1865. I looked down on the cold, harsh grey landscape and thought of them trying to eke out a living from that frozen earth. Powered flight was still nearly four decades from being a reality in 1865 and now here I was, their descendant, speeding through the air at 30,000 feet and Mach 0.86 in a four-engined giant. They could never have imagined such a thing and yet by the next sunrise, I would be in Hong Kong.

CHAPTER SEVENTEEN
SOUTHERN LIGHTS.

F ar from the cold northern extremes of the Kingdom of Prussia, the Qantas 747-400 also plied its trade at the southern fringes of the planet. From Sydney we would fly to the South African city of Johannesburg, heading west and chasing the sun in what felt like the longest day. A day that could witness the extremes of bushfires and ice bergs as well as wealth and poverty.

Before I began flying and learned of "Great Circle Routes", like most people, I had expected the flight would head west to Africa via Perth in Western Australia. After all, that was the route when my father flew the Super Constellation. But I was very wrong.

The shortest distance to Johannesburg from Sydney was almost "under" the planet and not "across" it and the first capital city we would overfly would be Melbourne, followed shortly thereafter by Hobart. This flight was southbound to latitudes approaching 60 degrees south, near the Antarctic Circle. Consequently, when our flight plan package was examined preflight, it included a fuel temperature table, just as it had when we flew at the northern extremes between Hong Kong and London. However, the terrain was not an issue across the Indian and Southern oceans.

The added benefit of tracking so far south was to remain clear of the eastbound jet stream. This stream of high-speed air was a significant headwind that would significantly increase our flight time and fuel burn. Even so, the flight time would be over thirteen hours, although we would reap the benefit of the jet stream for a fast flight home in a few days.

As the process dictated, the final load sheet was the last piece of documentation to arrive on the flight deck. This detailed not only the total weight of the aircraft, passengers, cargo, and fuel but considered that it had all been loaded "in balance." When an aircraft is loaded, its weight needs to be considered from two perspectives. Firstly, is the aircraft's total weight below its maximum weight for the various phases of flight. It may be limited structurally for taxi, take-off and/or landing, its airframe unable to bear a greater load with adequate safety margins. In turn, the performance of the aircraft may be restricted through a range of factors, from its engines' power output to the length of the runway to the air temperature and the elevation of the airfield above sea level. Johannesburg was a case in point being 5,500 feet above sea level and subject to warm summer days like Australia.

However, even if the physical weight of the aircraft met all of the structural and performance limits, there was another important aspect of the aircraft's weight to consider – how that weight was distributed or its "balance." Consider the see-saw. With a child of equal weight sitting at each end, the plank of the see-saw may well sit steady, in the middle, in balance. Should a large adult sit at one end, the see-saw will now tip and no longer be in balance. The issue of balance is a serious consideration in an aircraft and on the ground, if all the passengers congregate in the rear of the airliner cabin and cargo is only placed in the rear cargo bays, some large aircraft can tip onto their tail – like the see-saw.

Johannesburg was known for storms developing without notice in the afternoon, so crews inherently opted to carry enough fuel to "hold" until the weather cleared, or enough fuel to proceed to another airfield. This equated to a full fuel load and further consideration of the aircraft's "balance" because at the tail-end of its "see-saw" the Boeing 747-400 carried 10,000 kg of fuel in its horizontal tailplane – the stabiliser.

With the final load sheet checked and its details entered into the Flight Management Computer, the doors were closed, and we pushed back from the terminal. From Sydney, we flew over familiar territory from my days flying domestic sectors. Melbourne went by, followed by the Bass Strait and Flinders Island and onto Hobart, soon the most southern tip of the Apple Isle was behind us, and our trek overwater began.

Most of my hours spent over the Pacific Ocean were by night, but the flight to Johannesburg was entirely in daylight, with mile upon mile of ocean ahead. The Southern Ocean encircles Antarctica and officially begins at 60 degrees South latitude. We didn't always venture that far south on that flight, but we did fly far enough south to see icebergs with jagged peaks, floating in random formations. Their brilliant white surface was in stark contrast to the deep, dark frigid blue waters that surrounded them.

Mid-flight, Heard Island came into view out to the left-hand side of the aircraft. The most remote Australian Territory, Heard Island boasts a peak higher than Mount Kosciuszko and an active volcano. Cold and isolated, it hosted a sealing operation in the 19th century, and I wondered what such an existence would've been like - wild, wet, and windswept.

Beyond the mid-point, we rose through the latitudes towards Johannesburg. Descending over the coast and heading inland, I was struck by the similarity to the dry greens and browns of the Australian landscape. We stepped left and right about towering cumulus clouds to ensure a smooth ride for our passengers, but the clouds had yet to mature into full-blown storms, allowing our arrival to be on schedule at 3 pm on the same day, even though my body knew it was 11 pm back home. The joys of jet lag.

The drive to the hotel in an upmarket section of Johannesburg was always a poignant reminder of the extremes in our world. The crew bus would stop at traffic lights and people would walk along the road begging for money from the stationary vehicles. Some would offer dancing as entertainment and an incentive to contribute.

Approaching the hotel, residential areas had high walls, topped with razor wire, their mansions peeking above the fence line. Yet on the footpath outside, people sat barefoot in the dirt with torn shirts and a few meagre belongings. I wasn't naïve, I knew that wealth had extremes, but I had never seen them side by side in such a fashion.

We had been briefed about personal safety when moving about Johannesburg and that cramped my usual desire to explore. The layovers were now shorter, too short to venture into the back blocks on a safari tour, much to my chagrin. Still, I managed to safely navigate a path to an impressive military museum with artefacts dating back to the Boer War. On another flight, I was driven to Rand Airport to be shown a retired South African Airways 747 that stood as a gate guard to a museum.

Another ritual for the crew was to dine at one of the various restaurants where steaks were the meal of choice. Johannesburg is known for catering to carnivores with the most superbly cooked range of meats and every trip, flight crew and cabin crew could be found dining out in numbers. This unity also added an element of safety returning to the hotel. I never had any issues regarding my safety, although on one occasion I did realise that I was standing at a pedestrian crossing, next to a chap holding a machete. I smiled. He smiled. No problem.

To counter the jet lag, I often felt in Johannesburg, I kept my body clock close to Sydney time and rose at 3 am to go to the gym. I would return to my room and work on my master's degree or draft an article for a magazine. A sizeable breakfast at Doppio's Cafe, an early dinner and early to bed before rising at 3 am and working off all the food that I'd consumed. It was a strange system, but it worked for me.

The return flight east to Sydney differed in several ways. Departing in the evening, we would encounter nightfall soon afterwards, experience a brief night and arrive in Sydney in the afternoon of the following day. Importantly, the flight time was significantly shorter as we remained further north and surfed the jet stream home. Depending on the season, this could shave two hours off the time it had taken to fly to Johannesburg.

That short night often provided an amazing light show, the Aurora Australis, or "Southern Lights." The sister of the famed "Northern Lights" of the northern hemisphere, Aurora Australis is visible when charged particles stream from the sun on a solar wind and are drawn towards the north and south poles by the poles' stronger magnetic fields. On striking our atmosphere they release energy which manifests as a magnificent light show in the polar regions.

That night the glowing green curtain of the Southern Lights was in full force. Rhythmically waving as if concealing a theatre's stage but blown by a light wind. I drew out my camera to capture the amazing light show but I found the light to be insufficient and even if I had captured the image, no device could retain the sense of wonder I experienced.

In time the curtains parted, and dawn began to emerge ahead. Green was replaced by orange, darkness by light and night by day. I reflected on the past few days and the world that I had witnessed. From icebergs and isolated islands to the hot, brown countryside of South Africa. Long days and short nights, an amazing sunrise, and the Southern Lights. Wealth and poverty.

I had covered half of the earth and seen the multiple faces of the planet, the skies, and the people, perched on the flight deck of the 747.

I would be home soon, but I would never forget the feeling. I was one of the most fortunate people alive.

CHAPTER EIGHTEEN
IF THESE WALLS COULD SPEAK.

My first arrival into Frankfurt introduced me to my first "go around" in the 747. At the end of a long night, still in darkness and buffeted by howling winds, it was not the way that most flights were concluded but in aviation, you are trained to expect the unexpected.

Everything was set. We had the flaps fully extended, the landing gear down and the checklists completed. Runway 25 Centre lay ahead, its lights brilliant in the pre-dawn. A strong wind was blowing from our right and this landing would be close to the limits for the aircraft but nothing that wasn't regularly trained for in the simulator.

Approaching in a strong crosswind, the aircraft would weathercock into the wind and for a behemoth like the 747, that placed the flight deck outside of the alignment of the runway. Just before touchdown, the timely use of the rudder would yaw the aircraft straight to align with the runway and the landing would be completed. A challenge for the captain but he had done it all before many times.

An uneasy feeling began to creep across the crew. Another behemoth, a United States Air Force (USAF) C-5 Galaxy transport aircraft had been given clearance to line up on the runway we were rapidly approaching.

"Qantas 5, can you sidestep to runway 25 Left?"

The air traffic controller seemed unphased.

At this late stage in the approach with the wind blowing from our right, there was no way that we could change runways and meet the requirements of a "stable approach" which were not merely policy but the key to a safe approach and landing.

"Unable" The captain uttered a single word to the first officer.

"Qantas 5. Negative. Going around." The intent was conveyed to the controller.

The captain pushed one of the Take-Off/Go Around (TOGA) buttons just ahead of the thrust levers, summoning the engines to increase thrust and the nose of the aircraft to rise to a climbing attitude.

"Flaps 20." The captain called and the first officer obeyed.

"Positive rate." The F/O advised that the aircraft was now climbing.

"Gear Up" The F/O obeyed again and selected the landing gear to retract.

The calm end to the night had now become extremely busy.

"Require immediate right turn to return to land." The captain called and the F/O relayed.

While the aircraft had arrived with the legally required fuel in the tanks, this was not the time to be wandering around the sky without a plan. The rising of the nose and the sloshing of the fuel in the tanks caused the fuel low-pressure lights to blink, reinforcing the validity of the captain's plan for an immediate return.

Over the next ten minutes, checks were completed, passengers informed, the approach entered into the FMC, the procedure briefed again in an abbreviated fashion and the aircraft turned towards the airport, progressively extending flaps in anticipation of the landing. Soon we were back where we had begun - flaps fully extended, the landing gear down and the checklists completed, Runway 25 Centre ahead. This time there were no surprises beyond the challenge of the crosswind landing, although some unkind words were uttered about the air traffic controller a little later.

We were conveyed to our hotel in Mainz which sat on the banks of the Rhine River, around 40km from Frankfurt. Once again, I had to pinch myself as to where I was and how I came to be there. I had visited Frankfurt once before with Kirrily when she had been flying the

747 and that had been a trip to remember. We had backpacked to Burg Gutenfels, a medieval castle built upon a hillside in 1220, overlooking vineyards and another section of the Rhine River. We had engaged the caretaker in conversation and when he learned that we were pilots, shared that he had previously been a pilot, quietly adding, ".... during the war."

He had flown a range of fighters for the Luftwaffe but elaborated very little. Instead, he showed us to our room, a simple room with stone walls and centuries of history. We were the only guests, so he warned us that if we heard voices in the night, not to be alarmed as the castle was also used by NATO military staff for meetings with minimal notice.

Dinner was served in the grand main hall where Kirrily and I kept our voices low as the echoes were significant. The wine was a Rhine Riesling that was actually grown on the Rhine River and cellared in the castle. We feasted on the cold cheese and sausage before sitting by a small Juliet balcony overlooking the river. Very romantic.

On this trip I was on my own in Frankfurt, so the romance wasn't quite the same as I set out to explore Mainz. The city had been founded by the Romans in the first century BC and remnants of their time were still present, including ancient ships discovered in the 1980s that were the centrepiece of a seafaring museum. Everywhere the architecture reflected the layers of history that had been progressively laid on the city. The town square was bathed in sunshine, surrounded by grand architecture, markers, and monuments, I was in my realm. Among the monuments was a tribute to Johann Gutenberg, the inventor of the 15th Century Gutenberg printing press that is credited with spreading literacy and education across Europe through the cheaper mass production of books.

The town's history also had a darker side. I ventured by the former headquarters of the Gestapo where interrogations had taken place during the war, while other buildings still bore the scars of bombing and strafing. Some landmarks had survived for centuries, while others had not.

Although this flight had arrived in the middle of summer, Frankfurt could be a frozen city, too. Later that year I would undertake my first preflight "walkaround" of an aircraft in snow and witnessed the process by which the aircraft's surface was cleared of any snow, or ice that could contaminate the aircraft and impede its ability to take-off. The German ground crew were well practised in the process, spraying the required fluids to guard against any contamination before the flight, while we would taxi without delay following the process and "run-up" the engines before take-off.

For now, the skies were clear and the day before we left, I had crammed into the town square with the crew and the residents of Mainz to witness the World Cup final, broadcast across a huge screen. Unfortunately, the German side lost to Brazil 2-0 but like every moment of my time in Germany, it was an education.

Our departure was uneventful compared to the early morning go-around on our arrival at Frankfurt a few days before. Now it was another city fading from my view and my eyes now focused ahead on the multiple aircraft that filled the skies. We moved into our routine of completing the flight plan, assembling updated weather, monitoring the aircraft, and making an announcement to the passengers before they drifted off to sleep.

The idea of sleep appealed to me, so I volunteered to take the first rest break and left the flight deck to settle in my coat cupboard accommodation. Seat reclined, uniform shirt hung up and lights extinguished, I closed my eyes and let the sound of the airflow outside ease me into sleep while thousands of feet below, beneath the belly of the aircraft, the historic fields of Europe slipped away.

CHAPTER NINETEEN
THE CITY OF ANGELS.

Bidding for preferred trips was a function of how long you had been in the company. I had been on the front edge of a recruitment wave in the wake of the Ansett collapse, so I moved up the bidding totem pole reasonable quickly. With a young family and my wife who was also a pilot, the priority shifted to shorter trips, rather than the long haul to European ports. The solution lay across the Pacific in the city of angels, Los Angeles.

Some found the long hours of darkness bound for America tedious and it was a reservation that I shared when I first began flying international routes. However, there were many ways to remain occupied. Monitoring the aircraft and maintaining communications and a flight log were some core elements but there are others.

Along the way the crew would continually assess a plan of action should a range of emergencies occur at any given moment. A depressurisation that called for a descent to a lower altitude, an engine failure, or the destination becoming fog bound and requiring an alternate airport to be found. To maintain this level of situational awareness, weather conditions at a range of airports were updated through the night, primarily through printouts derived through an automated system but sometimes "old school" through scratchy HF radio, listening to periodic broadcasts known as VOLMETs.

The various strategies were supported by pre-planned data that filled the latter pages of the flight plan, outlining the fuel, time, and distance to divert in flight. These plans highlighted the waypoints where one option gave way to a new airport that was now closer. These were presented as Decision Points or DPs. Mingled with the conversation, thoughts of the world outside, the night sky, the management of the aircraft made the hours pass more quickly than one might expect. Even so, by the time the sun edged above the horizon and the United States drew near, the crew were more than ready to disembark once the aircraft had been safely parked.

Approaching the west coast was met with increasing nautical traffic on the ocean below, ranging from supertankers to naval vessels and inturn pleasure craft as Santa Catalina Island came into view on our descent. Crossing the coast, a left turn would be made towards Los Angeles International Airport (LAX), although a careful eye would also be cast to the right as a long queue of other descending inbound aircraft filled the sky to the south. Dots in the sky appeared as tiny white diamonds on our navigation displays that detailed their relative position.

The density of the traffic combined with the rapid-fire air traffic control instructions made for a very busy arrival with some of those inbound aircraft flying parallel to us to one of LAX's other runways.

Below and to the left, the Queen Mary could be seen anchored at Long Beach where it was now a tourist attraction, close to a massive dome that once housed Howard Hughes' aircraft the Hercules – better known as the "Spruce Goose." To the right, the Hollywood sign could just be seen on a clear day, although too often Los Angeles was blanketed in a layer of haze.

On final approach, four parallel runways lay ahead with two on either side of the main airport complex. We usually landed to the left, or west, on the "25 complex".

A clearance to land could be granted with aircraft still ahead on the runway, such was the amount of air traffic flowing through the American west coast port. Once landed, the runway was vacated promptly but not so hurriedly as to exit and infringe a nearby parallel runway.

The arrival may have been fast-paced but clearance through immigration and customs was always slow. Many crew, me included, only carried a wheelie bag rather than checking in a suitcase. However, there were those occasions when a shopping expedition was planned that justified far more capacity.

For most of my time on the 747, we were accommodated at Pasadena, and I loved the town. There was no shortage of entertainment ranging from the Pasadena Playhouse where the likes of Dustin Hoffman and Gene Hackman, made their acting debut. A small independent theatre, the best array of aviation magazines at the newsagent and fantastic restaurants added to my entertainment. And if I wanted to escape further, a hire car to Chino Airport was close at hand.

Chino was the home of two aviation museums and a swarm of airworthy warbirds that were frequently displayed at air shows. And every visit began with breakfast at "Flo's Diner." Tucked between hangars and huts Flo's was an absolute must for any visit to the airfield. Behind the old screen door, the waitresses hustled about with pots of coffee as jacketed pilots, engineers, enthusiasts, and tourists hunched over the nearby counter. The coffee was black, the eggs were over-easy, and the menu kept cardiologists in business. The walls were all but hidden by yellowing wartime posters that proclaimed support for 'Our Boys' and an array of photos that portrayed long-gone men and machines. The background hum of conversation sat well with the bustle of laden trays and created an atmosphere that had remained unchanged for more than half a century. Flo's was more about character than cuisine.

On one occasion, my flight didn't terminate in Los Angeles as I had been called out on Boxing Day to fly to LAX as a passenger. It was the midst of the American winter and snow had been forecast for the east coast, notably New York. The 747 normally flew the return flight to John F. Kennedy Airport with two pilots but when the weather was forecast for the east coast, an additional pilot was sent to assist, particularly as lengthy delays could see the flight cancelled if the two crew ran out of legal duty time. A third pilot extended this duty time.

Having never been to JFK previously, I studied the books and charts on the way over to Los Angeles before joining the crew a day later. The cross-country flight from the west to east coast took about five hours and took in amazing scenery. I was also amazed by the number of runways across the United States – they were everywhere. Large and small, civil and military. It seemed that every few miles another strip of cleared land or asphalt welcomed aircraft and I wondered what it would involve if I were to fly across the country in a biplane at some future date. I could dream.

From rugged ranges on the west coast to vast inland plains, we tracked northeast towards Chicago and the Great Lakes before heading east to New York. I had heard a great deal about the Canarsie approach into JFK and discussed it with the crew on the flight over. The approach passed over the Canarsie radio beacon and hugged the shoreline over parkland that bordered a small bay before a gradual descending right turn aligned the aircraft with the runway. The last section of the manoeuvre was hand flown visually and could be complicated by prevailing winds.

On the night of our arrival, the sky was clear and the winds light, making for a spectacular view of the New York skyline. On the flight deck, the captain guided the giant 747 along the shore and around the corner, a line of flashing strobe lights indicating the extended centreline of the runway. The wings were rolled level around five hundred feet above the ground and the 747 was brought gently to earth.

My time in New York was non-stop. My best friend had moved to the city just before 9/11 and even witnessed the events of that day. I was introduced to real New York pizza and visited the Statue of Liberty and Ellis Island, where so many immigrants had first encountered America.

Our hotel was on Times Square and with a departure on New Year's Eve, the city was abuzz, although the heightened threat of a terrorist attack was being openly raised on media outlets. Fortunately, no such event occurred, and I had a wonderful time in New York. And never saw a cloud in the sky – let alone any snow.

While crossing the United States took five hours, returning to Australia from the west coast was substantially longer. Prevailing headwinds made the trip home slower and varied between thirteen and fifteen hours, depending on whether your destination was Sydney, Brisbane or the furthest port, Melbourne. There were also sectors via

Auckland which permitted an overnight stop and the finest meal of mussels I had ever tasted and even the occasional Trans-Tasman cricket match.

The sector to Melbourne was close to the limit for the 747-400ER, particularly when the winds were against her. Consequently, a close eye was kept on the weather at Melbourne throughout the night and the aircraft's fuel state was equally monitored. Should the weather forecast turn foul and the need for extra holding fuel be required, the possibility of diverting to Avalon remained. However, Avalon was frequently not any better and another plan of attack needed to be initiated.

The tactic was known as a Technical Stop, or "Tech Stop". The stopover would have the passengers remain on board and the aircraft would be fuelled with minimal delay and the flight would continue to the planned destination. In the days before the ER, westbound Pacific crossings would occasionally land at Nadi, Fiji to "gas and go". Still, for the longer sector to Melbourne, a tech stop in Sydney was needed in rare instances to top up the fuel and safely deliver the passengers with minimal delay.

The Los Angeles sector remained one of my most common trips. In time our accommodation moved from Pasadena to downtown Los Angeles, although I still caught the train to my old stomping ground. Outside of business hours, downtown seemed abandoned and eerie and I only ventured out with the crew, or across the road to a hidden bar whose shelves were stacked with books and small corner tables for reading.

By this time, I had started writing consistently for a range of magazines and my time away was being used efficiently. From my desk, I could see the Hollywood sign on Mount Lee, and it seemed fitting as I pounded away at the keyboard. I was beginning to miss being in the control seat of an airliner, as much as I had enjoyed my ticket to the world. I had bid for a return to the 737 and with recruitment happening at Qantas, it seemed that a promotion was imminent but not before at least one more visit to my favourite city by the bay.

CHAPTER TWENTY
I LEFT MY HEART
IN SAN FRANCISCO.

The promotions had been published and after four years on the 747, I was back to the future and set to train on the Boeing 737, returning to domestic operations. There were some mixed feelings as my world had truly grown and my life made richer through my time on the 747. However, the pilot inside was bursting to break out. I had kept my hand in as a volunteer flying instructor for the Air Force Cadets and dawdling about in other light aircraft, including a biplane we owned for some time. However, the opportunity to fly the 737 again and its new variant, the Next Generation "800" was something that I was looking forward to. I just had some final boxes to tick.

In the same way that I had once travelled with Kirrily in her time on the 747, she had accompanied me on flights through the generosity of her parents volunteering to babysit our children. I had successfully bid for a flight that would have me in San Francisco for New Year's Eve and as I was leaving the fleet in the coming months, could not imagine a better farewell than to share that evening by the bay with my wife.

San Francisco had quickly become my favourite port when it returned to the Qantas 747 network earlier that year. It was an interesting arrival to parallel runways that had converging instrument approaches, meaning that the aircraft on your wing slowly grew closer as you drew nearer to the runway. Combined with aircraft arriving and departing on the crossing runway and being cleared to land along with aircraft ahead, San Francisco made for a busy airport.

Air Traffic control could sometimes leave you "high" above the ideal profile to fly the approach which was best countered by slowing down and extending flaps and if needed, landing gear. From this point, the aircraft could comfortably descend to regain the approach path, although that could be made interesting if the controller also wanted us to maintain a higher speed. Experience and anticipation were the best assets in this situation, and we almost expected to have to put in the effort to get back on profile relatively late in the approach.

San Francisco could be subjected to heavy fogs as moist air is drawn in from over the Pacific Ocean. Iconic images exist of the towers of the Golden Gate Bridge protruding from the white blanket enveloping the city. More prevalent in the summer months, we would always monitor the conditions carefully through the night with nearby Oakland, or Los Angeles viable options in the case of a diversion.

Our accommodation was close to the heart of the city and Union Square, offering a range of options at our doorstep. Cable cars rang their bells and climbed the steep hills that featured in so many Hollywood movies while cars crawled down Lombard Street, reputed to be the most winding street in the world.

Across the way was Alcatraz Island, its prison perched on its rocky outcrop and in clear view from the shores of the city. Despite the hardened criminals and harsh conditions of the prison, I suspected that the greatest torture may have been seeing freedom so close and yet so far. I caught the ferry and toured the facility, viewing its many cells and hearing of its many tales. In the gift shop, an ex-convict was signing copies of his book and I was reminded of my book signing as an author at Duxford and a very different setting.

Without a doubt, my favourite pastime was hiring a bike and riding across the Golden Gate Bridge. I would take the long way around to hire a bicycle, walking with my backpack past the ferry terminal and Fisherman's Wharf. From there I would follow the popular track to where the pathway met the roadway on the southern approach to the bridge. Pedestrians and bikes filled the dedicated route across the bridge where signs and bright yellow telephones offered last-minute assistance for those contemplating jumping from the bridge. Sadly, it was not an uncommon occurrence.

From the bridge the view was spectacular. Towering orange pillars and cables above and choppy waters below lapped at the base of Alcatraz. Boats great and small passed beneath the bridge as did the occasional helicopter. On completing the crossing, various options were available – a return crossing, a hill climb in parkland, or a visit to the small village of Sausalito and a return journey via the ferry.

On the New Year's trip, Kirrily and I opted for the latter, stopping for lunch by a pier and exploring the various specialty shops. We bought some gifts for the kids, and I purchased postcards and stamps. Ever since I had been flying the 747, I had sent postcards home in what was an "old school" tradition and gave our kids a thrill to receive mail – even if I frequently beat the postcards home.

As the ferry cut its way past Alcatraz and back to the city, swarms of massive gulls tailed the boat with tourists obligingly casting food in their direction until we docked and disembarked.

When New Year's Eve arrived, Kirrily had organised a table on the waterfront from where we could see the fireworks. We had been issued with appropriately ridiculous "Happy New Year" hats which we wore on the cable car and beyond as we made our way back to the hotel.

All too soon, we were back at the airport where Kirrily made her way to check-in, and I made my way to the briefing. The flight home was always longer than the sector to San Francisco due to the prevailing winds and a full fuel load was the order of the day.

As we flew home, I lay in the crew rest and contemplated what my time flying the 747 had truly meant. My career had been at its lowest point when Ansett had collapsed, and Qantas offered me a lifeline. I had been required to start over again as a junior pilot in a new airline but that had been to my advantage. The time away from home had allowed me to complete my master's degree and forge a second career as a writer of sorts. The professional insecurity I had felt in solely being a pilot was gone, bolstered by the other skill sets that I had gained.

More than anything, I had travelled farther and experienced more of the world than I could ever have imagined. From experiencing remnants of history at close quarters to experiencing cuisine that I'd never heard of. Meeting people of diverse cultures and realising how small my corner of the planet truly was. The sights, the scenery, the smells. My life was now much richer.

And then there was the aircraft that had taken me there, the Boeing 747-400. I had marvelled at its engineering for years, although I had never sought to fly it. The aircraft that Joe Sutter had "fathered" had changed the way we travelled and democratised the process. The hum of those four reliable engines through the night and the lullaby of the slipstream in the crew rest facility would soon be in my past. Another logbook was completed and another chapter closed in my career.

I was comfortable in my decision to return to the 737, although I knew there were aspects of my 747 life that I would miss. For the moment, I laid back in my darkened corner at the rear of the 747s upper deck and let the memories swirl and ease me to sleep as Sydney grew closer – mile by mile. Now, it was time for farewell to the 747 and thank you.

PART THREE
BACK TO THE FUTURE.

CHAPTER TWENTY-ONE
BACK TO THE FUTURE.

A lot can happen in a decade. Another child arrived to make our tally four and I had settled back into the routine of domestic flying on the 737, while Kirrily rose to be the most senior First Officer on the 767, operating its final farewell flight in 2014. Our lives had been a constant juggling of rosters to ensure that one of us was always home with the kids as they always remained our priority.

2014 also saw me accept a secondment to the Qantas subsidiary Jetstar, where I gained a command flying the Airbus A320 and A321. It had long been a career goal to become a captain and I had been tantalizingly close thirteen years earlier when Ansett had ceased operations. The hours were long, and the trips were all single-day trips and usually flying four sectors each day.

With the 767 retired and our children growing up fast, Kirrily at first took leave without pay and then moved to the role of Second Officer on the 747 on a part-time basis. There, her seniority would allow her to fly the exact trips she wanted and on the exact days she wanted, allowing her to work around my schedule and care for the kids. It was a sacrifice that I appreciated, and we both recognised it as a sound move.

Beyond flying, I had progressively written more content for a broader range of magazines and published several books. The spectre of being told that as a pilot I was "highly skilled but unemployable" following the failure of Ansett had now been cast aside. My writing had allowed me to fly in military aircraft, flight review numerous civilian aircraft and even travel to Spain and France to cover stories relating to Airbus.

With Qantas, I had been among the crews that operated a new and refined navigation system, known as RNP, into the beautiful New Zealand port of Queenstown. Home to the "Hobbits" in filming the "Lord of the Rings" trilogy, the flight path would weave among spectacular snow-covered peaks and across majestic waterways. I had also been fortunate to ferry a new Boeing 737-800 VH-VZT home from the factory in Seattle and while there visit the "Museum of Flight" where the first Boeing 747 was on display.

When the opportunity came to finally achieve a captaincy at Jetstar in 2014, I seized it. The endorsement training was in Southampton in England over six weeks in the company of other Qantas pilots who'd taken up the same posting. It was a strongly knit group from which many solid friendships were formed.

When the secondment ended in late 2017, a decision had to be made whether to remain at Jetstar permanently or to return to Qantas. Recruitment had been slow at Qantas, so the only real option was to return to the 737 fleet, however, the years of busy domestic flying had proven a difficult balance for family life and our four children were now reaching significant ages ranging from eight to fifteen. A decision had to be made.

I was content that my career goals had now been met, despite the various hurdles along the way. My priorities now lay squarely with the needs of my family. I had seen the benefits that Kirrily's seniority as a Second Officer had in bidding for a roster on the 747 and I would not be that far behind her in the queue on the Queen of the Skies. Increasingly, the best option seemed to be that I follow her lead and bid back to become a Second Officer on the 747. The aircraft was due to retire in a few years but that few years could prove to be a valuable time for all of us as a family.

The decision made, it needed to be approved by Qantas as I was stepping back from being a Qantas Group Captain, or senior 737 First

Officer, to the lower rank of Second Officer. It could be done but it was at the discretion of the company. In turn, we discussed the situation with management and to their credit and our gratitude, they approved my choice. I was returning to the 747.

By coincidence, I was scheduled to train on the 747 with a 737 First Officer who was also married to a pilot and had made the same request for the same reasons. Together, Luke and I had a combined experience level of more than 30,000 hours of flight time and had both previously been trained on the 747. We also lived nearby and shared the driving to training, using those hours on the road to revise our theory lessons and rehearse our simulator sessions.

It was a near-perfect situation for training and a process that could be trying was an absolute pleasure. We covered the familiar ground that we had studied years before and soon we were cleared back to the line. I had never anticipated returning to flying the long-haul routes and even less the opportunity to fly the Boeing 747. Now, I was on the verge of venturing to foreign lands once again and I was excited at the prospect.

There had been some changes at Qantas while I had been away flying the Airbus A320. On the surface, the most obvious difference was the white peaked cap, redesigned uniform wings and thinner bars on the epaulettes and jacket. The new-look had certainly been met with a mixed response in my absence.

Many of the captains that I had flown with previously had now retired, with Sandy Howard among that number. They were replaced by a newer generation, many of whom had made their way to the "Jumbo" via the 767 and had flown with Kirrily in her fifteen years on that aircraft.

At an operational level, the most significant change was the adoption of the iPad on the flight deck and the multiple purposes that it could serve. We had trialled a heavy digital "tough book" on the 737 before the iPad but it had previously been limited to the domestic fleet. Now pilots operating the 747 were sharing in the technology.

The iPad replaced many of the tasks that were previously achieved with pen and paper, notably performance calculations. Gone was the thick folder of airport tables to calculate power settings and take-off speeds, replaced by speedy computations following the entry of the relevant data. The requirement to cross-check results remained but the speed, accuracy and additional functions were very impressive.

Similarly, the paper airport and navigation charts were replaced with digital equivalents, able to have the route overlaid among other data. A weather app brought enroute weather to life in full colour, kilograms of company manuals were loaded on the iPad with a speedy search function. And for Second Officers, the endless paper flight plan was gone. Not only was it replaced, but on entering the departure time the intervals were automatically added to calculate an arrival time at the destination. There were many other functions too, making the iPad tablet a major leap forward in flight management and planning.

Qantas had received its first Airbus A380 in 2008 and the double-deck airliner was deployed on the European and Los Angeles routes. When I returned to the 747 fleet, Tokyo and Honolulu, Vancouver and the capital of Chile, Santiago, were now in its network. Johannesburg and Hong Kong remained 747 ports with the 787 Dreamliner soon to claim New York. Except for a 72-hour layover in Santiago, the trips were four to five days and were well suited to my family situation.

Despite my keenness to return to the 747 fleet, I knew that its days were numbered. The first 747-400, VH-OJA – "The City of Canberra" - had retired to the Historical Aircraft Restoration Society (HARS) Museum, south of Sydney a few years earlier in what was the shortest sector the 747 had undertaken, totalling a mere fifteen minutes. This was an extreme contrast to its record-breaking delivery flight in 1989 when it flew between London and Sydney non-stop. A flight that in 1919 took the Smith brothers nearly 28 days was achieved by VH-OJA in a little over 20 hours, eighty years later. It was a stark reminder of just how far aviation had advanced in a relatively brief time. The flight set the record for the longest non-stop flight for a commercial aircraft and without the benefits of air-to-air refuelling. OJA would not be alone as the Rolls-Royce powered 747-400s were progressively being retired, although not sharing the same fortunate fate as a preserved museum piece, they were destined to be retired to a distant graveyard in the United States.

To such a backdrop, I was determined to cherish every opportunity the 747 would undoubtedly offer. It had been the aircraft that had thrown me a lifeline when my career had faltered in the wake of the Ansett collapse and now it was stepping in again. When my first roster was published, I could not have been happier with my first destination. My old stomping ground, the city that I loved – San Francisco.

CHAPTER TWENTY-TWO
ON THE ROAD AGAIN.

As the driver kept his eyes on the road, I began to scroll through the iPad as we drew closer to the airport. Another advantage of the tablet was the ability to review the flight details and start to organise the appropriate mindset well in advance of the flight. The weather, notices to airmen (NOTAM), proposed flight plan and fuel load could all be considered with a tap and a swipe. Retraining on the 747 had an air of familiarity, however, there were certain aspects of the operation that had lapsed into distant memory. Having spent most of my career flying two-crew on domestic routes with four or five flight attendants, the sheer size of the preflight welcome seemed alien. As I walked through the terminal as one of four pilots, the team grew even further when we met the fourteen cabin crew members in the gate lounge. The ritual of introductions and handshakes were mixed with the formal details of flight time, weather conditions and other operational details.

The size of the flight deck was not a surprise as the simulator was identical, but I had forgotten how far above the tarmac the cockpit sat. Furthermore, as I walked around the outside of the aircraft as part of the preflight inspection, it was a much longer process than inspecting the 737 or A320. The red fin with its kangaroo reached high into the sky, the sweep of the wing and four large engines waited to settle into their rhythm.

The first take-off also jerked my memory into gear. As the engines spooled up to take-off thrust, the sound was distant, so far ahead was the flight deck. Similarly, the accelerating wheels and tyres rumbled with even the closest wheels, the nose gear, behind me, thirty feet and a layer of Business Class below. The ground roll before liftoff seemed to go on forever and while the no-go speed (V1) and the speed to become airborne, or rotate (Vr), were at times simultaneous on the smaller twin-engined jets, this was not the case on the 747. The split between V1 and Vr at heavy weights was around ten knots and, even though we were on the ground, the take-off could and would be safely continued in the event of a problem. And that lift-off speed could be over 300 km/h. I was tangibly reminded how everything to do with the 747 was on a grand scale.

The flight across the Pacific and the long dark hours were familiar, although the scratchy transmissions on the HF radio had been greatly reduced by a satellite-based system. Position reports and requests for weather diversions or climbs to a higher level were all conveyed through the FMC and the datalink system. Crossing the longitude of 140 West was the one frequency transfer through the night that was done by voice, not the datalink system. It made for a peaceful evening of monitoring the aircraft, the weather and the options should we need to divert.

When the time came for a rest break, it was back to my bunk in the coat cupboard once again. That was familiar. The slipstream sliding by with a whisper and the occasional ripple in the airflow rocking me to sleep. All too familiar was the horrid squeal of the wake-up call which was activated from the flight deck. The piercing sound was coupled with the lights bursting into life with a vengeance.

Having left the flight deck in darkness, creeping through the business class passengers on the upper deck, I returned with sunlight attempting to break in through the cracks of slightly opened window shades. Walking onto the flight deck I was blinded with the sun dead ahead.

The top of descent was approaching, and we gathered for a bite of breakfast and a briefing. The weather was fine and we were planning to land on Runway 28 Left. It had been more than ten years since I had left San Francisco and I felt genuine excitement to be there again. As the coastline passed beneath our wings and we began the left turn towards the airport, it didn't seem like a decade had elapsed. Even at altitude, I was reminded of what I enjoyed about international flying. The different architecture, the tones of nature, topography, and landmarks. And of course, the Golden Gate Bridge and Alcatraz Island in the distance.

The airport was still as congested with traffic on the crossing runways and near-parallel arrivals edging closer to our right-hand side. We were cleared to land, and the crew confirmed the clearance verbally. Runway 28 Left drew closer and I recalled that it had been the scene of the Asiana Boeing 777 crash only a few years before. Like all accidents, many lessons had been learned in the aftermath.

We landed uneventfully and taxied to our gate past long queues of aircraft waiting to depart. Every airline and type of aircraft imaginable was waiting their turn and I was reminded how expansive airline operations were beyond Australia's relatively small network. Entering our parking apron, the appropriate radio frequency was set, and we were greeted with "Ahoy!" by the ramp controller. It was a friendly greeting that I came to know with each arrival and departure from San Francisco.

In town, I hit the ground running, assisted by a map and instructions from Kirrily who knew the city well. Our new hotel on Bush Street was fantastic and the Beanstalk Café was located nearby for the morning brew. Then it was off for my traditional walk past the ferry terminal to Fisherman's Wharf and a bike ride over the bridge. It all felt like home.

When the next day arrived, there was a little adventure that I had organised before leaving Sydney. I had always wanted to overfly the city in a helicopter but never had the opportunity previously, so I was determined to make it happen.

I had managed to organise the best seat in the house - up front and alongside the pilot. Ron Carter was a seasoned aviator with 13,000 hours and having gained the 'thumbs up' from his passengers, eased the Bell 407 into the air from the Sausalito helipad. One thing that

I've always enjoyed about helicopters is the immediacy of the flying. There is no taxing along the ground, once you had decided to move in a helicopter, from that moment, you were flying.

Through the clear nose section beneath my feet, I saw the helipad fall away before we departed to the west and over the hills towards the Pacific Ocean, levelling out at 2,000 feet. Ron pointed out features ranging from old fortifications to the magnificent Golden Gate Bridge. Crossing the water, we descended as we approached the southern shore, before turning back towards the bridge. The day was magnificent, clear, and not a puff of wind.

He lowered the nose of the Bell and descended in a smooth arc before sweeping beneath the historic bridge, the water rushing below the helicopter's skids. Then, with minimal effort, the helicopter pitched up into a climbing left turn and back over the Golden Gate. Wow!

From there we tracked back towards the city, and I noted historic landmarks, the stadium that the San Francisco Giants baseball team called home, Fisherman's Wharf, the Bay Bridge to Oakland and Alcatraz. Thirty minutes had passed all too soon, and we returned to the Sausalito helipad with a descending turn and a gentle touchdown. I disembarked and made my way clear of the spinning rotor before turning and grabbing one last photo of the gleaming red helicopter, then the ground staff ushered me into position for a 'selfie.' Bucket list – ticked.

San Francisco was everything I remembered and more. There were baseball games to watch, museums to visit and many more crossings of the Golden Gate to be ridden. I knew that I'd be back again soon and with the days of the 747 numbered, I was determined to squeeze every drop out of the time that this giant of the sky would afford me.

CHAPTER TWENTY-THREE
LAND OF THE RISING SUN.

Despite having travelled extensively, there had been one destination that had evaded me – Japan. Tokyo had been brought into the 747's network since I was last flying internationally, and the city had personal significance. Following the end of World War Two, my father had been one of the first troops to land in Japan, having sailed there directly from New Guinea where he had served as a commando. He had been stationed at Hiroshima only a few months after the devastation of the atomic bomb but had also spent time in Tokyo. I had grainy photographs of troops, temples, and other buildings that I yearned to visit. The 747 presented me with the opportunity.

The flight to Tokyo was a quick, 3-day trip, flying through the night on both sectors. With a flight time of eight hours, the flight crew consisted of three pilots, and it was an accepted tradition for the Second Officer to take the first break of a couple of hours. With only three crew, my usual aft crew rest facility was offered to the upstairs flight attendants, and I settled into the crew rest at the rear of the flight deck.

By the time that I came back "on watch," northern Australia was just behind us, and New Guinea lay ahead in the darkness. The lights of Port Moresby glowed, and my mind was cast back to my time flying there before the airlines. Abbreviations on the 747's moving map display conjured images in my mind's eye. Gurney, Girua, Nadzab, Wewak and Manus Island to the north. All were places that I had flown to, some still possessing runways covered in Pieced Steel Planking, or PSP, which had been laid down during the war.

In the darkness below, I knew the peaks of the Owen Stanley Ranges reached skyward and among the jungles of New Guinea were tracks where my father had fought, and his friends had fallen.

Hour after hour, the islands of the Pacific war came and went. Guam, Tinian - from where the "Enola Gay" flew with its atomic payload, Saipan, and the black sands of Iwo Jima. Waypoints on a digital map to me, the resting place of thousands from another time. I longed for daylight to see those islands.

When dawn finally came, we were nearly at our destination and in the winter months, the arrival would indeed be in darkness. Airport curfews normally exist within the hours of the night, but Haneda Airport in Tokyo had a different type of "reverse curfew." We had to land in the early morning before a cut-off time to avoid the hefty landing fees associated with the airport's peak hour.

By now the first rays of daylight radiated out from the horizon like the Japanese flag from a bygone era and in the distance, Mount Fuji rose to meet the clouds. Even so, the runway lights blazed brightly as the daylight had yet to reach ground level with full strength as the 747 eased over the runway threshold and back to earth.

While some would head straight to bed on our arrival at the hotel, I always chose to keep moving. Like Hong Kong, Tokyo was a bustling city that was a ghost town in the early morning. I would walk down the main promenade, the Ginza, where shops and neon signs rose to the sky but in these hours, few people were to be seen. An occasional store would be changing its window display, guarded by multiple security guards in high visibility vests, with helmets and white gloves.

From there I would venture to the Imperial Palace, where the emperor resided, surrounded by a moat and stone walls. To circumnav-igate the palace was a five-kilometre walk and I learned that the local population did not take kindly to those who walked in the opposite direction to the convention. At times, the palace grounds were open to the public and ancient footings and incredible gardens could be experienced at close quarters.

My interest came from the black and white photos that I had in my pocket. I tried to recreate where my father had been standing when he snapped the images more than 70 years before. I found the small copper-topped guardhouses where he stood on duty with his white webbing belt and gaiters and bayonet fixed to the muzzle of his rifle.

I positioned at the top of a massive pathway and looked in the same direction that he aimed his camera as the building still stood today. I followed in his footsteps to reach the entrance of the building to learn that it was the post-war headquarters of General Douglas Macarthur. I was further intrigued to find that floor after floor had been preserved as they had been in the aftermath of the war, from the polished floors of the boardroom to the lounge areas, complete with period furniture and timepieces tick-tocking upon the walls. It was a hidden gem of history that was anonymous to the passer-by outside.

The extensive amount of walking during the layover always left me tired and ready for sleep before the inevitable call to duty rang through on the hotel phone. We would meet in the foyer and the extremely polite driver would convey us to Haneda Airport, our iPads glowing in the darkness with flight plans and fuel calculations.

In walking around the aircraft and pushing back from the terminal, the aircraft was surrounded by a swarm of ground crew going about their work in the most efficient manner. Crisp white overalls, glowing vests and hard hats were the order of the day as men with lit red batons walked our wingtips to ensure adequate clearance was maintained.

The taxi out to take-off from Runway 05 was extensive and entailed crossing the main runway complex and a taxiway that stood on pillars elevated above the water. The runway had been built on reclaimed land in recent years and saw arriving aircraft pass low overhead and dictated the timing of a take-off clearance.

At 2,500 metres, Runway 05 was one of the shorter runways from which the Qantas 747-400 departed. The disturbed air floating down from the arriving aircraft could also cause the airspeed to flicker as the 747 accelerated down the runway. This was always briefed for awareness, as it could cause some concern to a newcomer like me.

Once airborne into the night sky, we were held down at a low altitude as a stream of aircraft descended towards Haneda in the opposite direction to our flight path. One by one, their lights would grow closer and sweep by with a rush, our TCAS system indicating their distance away and vertical separation. In time, there would be a gap in proceedings, and we would climb to our cruise level, and I would take the first break.

Guam would be out the window when I returned, along with a typical line of tropical storms that we would give a wide berth to provide our passengers with a night of undisturbed sleep. New Guinea would be beneath us when the dawn approached and as Australia loomed, so did the sun. At the end of another night, we would return to the harbour city, its day just beginning, and we were home once more.

CHAPTER TWENTY-FOUR
NORTH TO VANCOUVER.

When departing Sydney off the northern runway to set course over the Pacific, there was a preference to turn right and head east from the outset. The published procedure did not offer this, particularly as there was a parallel runway in that direction, however, if traffic permitted, the Sydney controllers were always obliging. This early turn did more than save fuel and time but offered the passengers a scenic pass of Sydney Harbour, the bridge, and the Opera House. From there the departure would steam out through the heads and climb away. It was a wonderful way to farewell Sydney.

At the northern end of the sector to Vancouver, the daytime arrival could also be scenic. In the distance to the south, Mount St. Helens could be seen reaching skyward, while to the north a line of snow-capped peaks painted the horizon. The waterways surrounding Vancouver hosted vessels of all shapes and sizes, while the logs of the lumber industry floated down rivers in mass formations. As the 747 slowed and descended to circuit height, the city skyline passed by to the left before a sweeping left turn would position the aircraft on its final approach.

The seasons made a significant difference to the context of the arrival, from a crystal-clear day to a dark evening with wild winds and heavy rain. One such night the wind blew so strongly out of the south that it exceeded the crosswind limit for the 747, preventing the aircraft from landing on the usual 3,300-metre runway. However, Vancouver possessed a much shorter 2,200m runway that was aligned into the wind.

We independently calculated how much runway was required at our landing weight and with the assistance of a strong headwind, the 747 could comfortably land on the "cross runway". The passengers and crew were advised to be seated and the fasten seat belts sign was illuminated early in the descent in anticipation of a rough ride down low due to the wind. The turbulence arrived on cue as the captain, Marty Hart, navigated the Boeing to the north of the airport to turn back for a landing on Runway 13. Bounced and buffeted, the 747 rode the lumps and bumps impressively as it came around for the final approach.

The headwind was so strong that the aircraft seemed to be closing on the airfield at a snail's pace, the runway lights hardly growing closer between swipes of the wiper blades. The autopilot and autothrottle were working at capacity with the gusting winds until Marty disengaged them, preferring to fly the aircraft by hand. There was still a notable crosswind but far less than would have been encountered on the longer runway.

Slowly we approached the threshold with Marty working hard at the controls. Soon the approach lights slid beneath and then the runway's threshold. He squeezed in rudder to bring the nose of the aircraft to bear and in the most trying of conditions, the aircraft smoothly flew onto the runway, still buffeted by the wind and slowing to a halt with plenty of runway to spare. It was an impressive effort and Marty's night wasn't over. He had tickets to the ice hockey.

The view from the hotel could present a spectacular view of peaks and valleys or be enveloped in low cloud. Similarly, on a fine day, the riding paths could wend through Stanley Park where fare and fruit could be purchased at vibrant markets. On those cool, grey days, a cozy corner by the waterfront was also a pleasant way to pass an afternoon.

As a city, the waterways of Vancouver were always busy. Kirrily and I had crewed a flight together in the middle of a Northern summer, as her parents had kindly offered to stay with the "grandkids". On that trip, our room overlooked a floatplane base where aircraft came and went with regularity, adhering to a timetable reminiscent of a rail network. After all, the floatplane was the mode of transport in these parts. And when the aircraft returned, they docked on the pier with finesses, at times moving their propellers into reverse pitch to back into their assigned place. It was fascinating to watch, so we booked a flight for the next day.

The waterfront at Vancouver was lined with restaurants, coffee shops, and floatplanes. Commuters travelling to work cued alongside tourists like us taking to the skies to a dramatic backdrop of snow-capped mountains, that defied summer's climate. There was activity in every direction beyond the constant take-offs and landings that could be seen in the distance. Closer to shore, a range of aircraft such as the de Havilland Otters and Beavers mingled with Cessna Caravans as they taxied one behind the other in formation atop huge floats and along unseen taxiways of emerald water. At the dockside teams of 'ground crew', wearing lifejackets, secured recently arrived aircraft, before assisting passengers to disembark and refuelling the high-winged fleet for their next sortie.

Our pilot was a veteran of floatplane operations with decades of experience, from Canada to Fiji. Before we left the terminal, he briefed us and two other passengers on our aircraft and the operation of our lifejackets, should they be needed. We then made our way down the long wooden ramp to the docks and where our single-engined de Havilland DHC-2 'Beaver' waited.

Our aircraft was registered C-FZZJ and was immaculate in its appearance. The engine cowling was squeaky-clean and the condition of the paint was equally impressive. Stepping from the dock to the float and into the aircraft, its interior was spotless with leather seats, customised with an embroidered 'deHavilland Canada' logo. I moved through to the front seat, and although it was void of a control column and rudder pedals on my side, the outlook over the Pratt and Whitney radial engine was wonderful.

We left the dockside and joined a queue of taxiing floatplanes, our transit mixed in with traditional water-borne traffic, from leisure boats to much larger vessels. Occasionally, we crossed their wake and gently pitch up and down until smooth water was regained once again. The air traffic controller's voice rattled off through my headsets and it was a true act of coordination to sequence both aircraft and boats in the same expanse of water.

We turned in the direction of the take-off run and smoothly the Pratt and Whitney engine was brought up to full power. We immediately sat higher in the water and the float outside my window threw out an impressive spray of white water. A few more bumps as we skipped across a vessel's wake and then we transformed from a water-dweller to a graceful bird of flight.

We levelled off and ahead lay the aqua-green pylons of the Lion's Gate Bridge - but the bridge was void of traffic except for one or two vehicles. (We would later learn on the news that there was a 'jumper' being 'talked down' at the time.) The city skyline was just behind us and yet with a gentle left turn and a climb to 4,500 feet, it was a vista of towering mountains, jagged rocky outcrops and heavily wooded slopes that confronted us. To each side, the terrain climbed even higher and despite being the peak of a northern summer, snow could be seen on the peaks in the direction of Whistler - a world-renowned ski resort.

The Beaver's instrument panel was painted light grey and hosted a traditional six-pack of flight instruments, old-style levers, knobs, fuel cocks and switches, offset by a lone modern convenience, a small moving map and GPS.

At all times a waterway was below, undoubtedly offering a forced landing field to the floatplane if needed. Previously unnoticed by my wandering eyes, there was a beautiful deep-green lake, not far inland from a steep incline and surrounded by tall pines on the near side and snow-tinged rising rocky peaks beyond. It was amazing, it was Lake Lovely, and it was our destination.

From a traditional standpoint, the approach gradient seemed steep, and the grey rock faces at the far end of the lake precluded a go-around - this is effectively a one-way airstrip and one shot at a landing. Down the steep approach, we continued, with the aim point steady in the windscreen until the deep-green water was just beneath the floats. The power was then smoothly retarded until our floats skimmed the water and the white spray was again being thrown up outside my window. Once on the water, the Beaver slowed rapidly, and we began to sit lower in the water.

We were surrounded by breathtaking beauty as we taxied around an arm in the lake to a small recess where the Beaver slowly glided to a halt before our pilot leapt onto the float and then onto the land to secure the aircraft. Lake Lovely was fed by a glacier and from November to June, the entire lake was frozen, and landings were not possible. We wandered about this hidden gem for fifteen minutes, taking photos and trekking about the rocks and snow. I could imagine camping here in this beautiful isolation, but I could also picture a grizzly bear emerging from the tree line.

All too soon, we carefully tread across the rocks and retraced our steps from the floats to our passenger seats. With a push from the pilot, we drifted away from the water's edge, and he climbed aboard and strapped in. The engine roared, the water spray returned, and we were accelerating, becoming airborne shortly before the lake's arm and banking around the corner for departure.

The trees whizzed by in the distance and the lake's edge lay ahead, also bounded by trees. With the lake sitting at 3,700 feet above sea level, our departure was more like a launch as the world dropped away sharply to the valley floor and the river below and we were soon 4,000 feet above the ground, having only climbed 300 feet.

Approaching Vancouver, the air traffic controllers voice responded to our inbound radio call, and we were number three in the landing sequence, with the two other aircraft spotted ahead. One touching down and one not far behind. In a continual sweeping right-hand arc, we descended towards the open patch of water between the scurrying vessels and their wake. This was not as steep as the descent into Lake Lovely and the world seemed to slowly rise to meet the Beaver until we ever so smoothly contacted the water and concluded our flight.

It was a flight to remember and was still fresh in our minds as Vancouver's lights faded away behind us and the 747 set course in the night sky for the long haul home. The Beaver and the 747 – two different aircraft at different ends of the spectrum and both remarkable in what they could undertake. Regardless of the aircraft, every time the earth fell away from the wheels or the floats, I felt fortunate that I had been granted the good fortune to fly.

CHAPTER TWENTY-FIVE
SOMETHING DIFFERENT.

The QANTAS 747s often performed charter flights beyond the extent of the network. From ferrying Olympic teams to and from the Games to the "Captain's Choice" tours which offered international travel in luxury to a range of destinations. In times of crisis, the 747 was also called upon to bring Australians home. Notably, in 1974 when QANTAS made history evacuating 674 passengers, along with twenty-three crew, from Darwin following the destruction of Cyclone Tracy – setting a world record for carrying the most passengers on board a Boeing 747.

I was fortunate to be a part of two extraordinary flights on the 747. The first was the incredible experience of overflying Antarctica. The second was a charity flight to raise much-needed funds for drought-stricken farmers, it was the Qantas Rural Aid Charity Flight.

The flight to Avalon Airport near Melbourne was so much more than 'just another sector.' With the twilight of the Qantas Boeing 747 quickly becoming a sunset, tickets on board the 'Jumbo' flight to the International Air Show were always destined to be popular with aviation enthusiasts, particularly those that loved the 747. Consequently, when the limited number of 150 seats went on sale for the appropriate cost of $747, they were sold in a matter of hours. However, weeks before the tickets had even been released, preparations for the flight had been taking place.

As the day had grown closer, communications continued to abound between the various departments, while the technical crew focused on the operational detail and flight safety. The aim was to showcase the 747 with an arrival overhead the runway in front of the crowd before flying a visual circuit and landing. While a straightforward manoeuvre, Avalon Airport had special airshow procedures in place and the timings were critical, requiring that the Boeing be on the ground before the airshow operations officially commenced.

Having volunteered to crew the flight, Captain Mark Kelly and First Officer Craig Allan honed the arrival procedure in the simulator, examining a series of options with due respect paid to safety, airspace restrictions and other operational constraints. Through a combination of discussions, briefings and flight simulations, a scenario was devised for each of the arrival options – landing to the south on Runway 18, or the more likely profile of landing on Runway 36, given the forecast of Avalon's hot, northerly breeze. Even with every detail covered, the dynamic nature of airline operations led to an aircraft change at the eleventh hour from VH-OEB to VH-OJU.

Captain Kelly then addressed the cabin crew, who had also donated their time to operate the flight, just as QANTAS had donated the aircraft. He emphasised the importance of safety on a flight that was undoubtedly full of excitement and a little different to the long sectors that the 747 normally undertook. He also highlighted that while the arrival may seem different, it was nothing out of the ordinary – it was simply a visual circuit.

With the final details submitted and the crew briefed, the minutes were counting down. With the passengers still busy bidding on auctions of memorabilia and enjoying the preflight entertainment, we made our way through the terminal to the farthest domestic gate and the lone bay that could accommodate the expanse of the 747. There we found 'OJU,' refuelling hose attached, but otherwise at the ready for the flight south.

On the flight deck, the priorities and procedures remained the same. Checklists, briefings, and panel scans flowed, only interrupted by the occasional question, or visit by a camera crew. Each time, we carefully retraced our steps and recommenced partially completed procedures to ensure the interruption did not result in an oversight.

The final paperwork was signed off and the final ground staff were disembarked. Doors closed, pushed back and engines started, the 747 was cleared to taxi. Photographers were perched on Shep's Mound as QF1360 passed by and it was apparent from the first transmission that Air Traffic Control (ATC) was aware of the nature of the flight and the importance of its arrival time into Avalon. With the cabin secure and the checklists completed, OJU lined up on the runway and shortly after Captain Kelly raised its nosewheel into the air, allowing the graceful airframe to take flight.

Low cloud filled the valleys in the Southern Highlands before Canberra poked its head through a layer of stratus. The First Officer busily programmed the Flight Management Computer (FMC) with the expected arrival and the captain briefed the descent, approach, and landing, just as he had done in the simulator in the days preceding the flight. As expected, the weather was hot and windy and favouring Runway 36.

To offer the crowd a view of the four-engined legend, the plan was to arrive at Avalon from the north as if flying an approach to Runway 18, albeit higher than the profile needed to land. On reaching the runway, Captain Kelly would turn right to position the aircraft parallel to the runway complex on a left downwind leg, before completing the circuit to land on Runway 36. It was a manoeuvre they had rehearsed, and that ATC was anticipating when they cleared QF1360 to commence descent.

As the destination grew ever closer and the aircraft lower, the surrounding scenery was a poignant reminder of the cause behind the flight. In every direction I could see that the landscape was brown, creek beds were little more than clay and the heat seemed to rise from the parched earth. As the 747's shadow clipped across the ground it seemed to offer the only relief from the harsh rays of the sun. The drought was hitting hard and those on the land deserved all the assistance that could be offered.

Reaching 1,500 feet, the 747 was flown slightly right of the runway centerline before continuing into a right turn as planned. Below the crowd pointed and cameras clicked and the queue of vehicles to enter the airshow was already winding on for kilometres.

The crew's focus alternated between configuring the aircraft, monitoring the instruments, and flying the visual approach with 'eyes outside.' Rolling onto 'final,' with landing gear and flaps extended and checklists completed, the 747 was cleared to land. As the radio altimeter counted down the feet, Captain Kelly eased back on the control column and thrust levers to lower the Boeing smoothly onto the runway. Lowering the nosewheel, the reverse thrust was deployed to idle.

Needing to turn around at the far end of the runway, the 747 rolled out, smoothly decelerating before backtracking in front of an enthusiastic crowd line. As she exited the runway and moved towards her parking space, the crowd moved with her and the admiration for the 'Queen of the Skies' was plain to see.

Slowing to enter the parking apron, the ground crew waved their batons, easing the Boeing 747-400 to a slow and gentle halt. One by one, fuel flow was cut to the engines and the giant turbofan engines spool down. Outside the crowd had gathered to see the 'Queen of the Skies,' while the view from the flight deck revealed multiple marquees and military hardware that included American F-22 Raptors and the Royal Australian Air Force's F-35 Lightning. The Qantas Rural Aid charity flight had arrived at the Australian International Air Show.

The passengers on the return flight from Avalon that afternoon were far more subdued, exhausted by a day of heat and excitement. However, my next charter flight was anything but hot, departing from Melbourne to the frozen continent, Antarctica.

CHAPTER TWENTY-SIX
MAGNIFICENT DESOLATION.

From 31,000 feet, it emerged ambiguously on the horizon. At first, one questioned whether it was a cloud bank. But soon the distinct and jagged profile of mountains put paid to any questions. The Boeing 747-400 speeding toward Cape Adare was a far cry from the wooden vessels that crept through the frigid waters in 1841 to first sight and name the peninsula. But while the craft may have changed, the landscape that loomed ahead had retained its unchanged majesty. It was Antarctica.

With sea vessels required to cross vast distances through frigid waters and pack ice, flight offered both a speedy and comfortable means of commercial transport to view Antarctica. In 1977, the first Qantas aircraft, a Boeing 747-238B, was chartered by Australian businessman, Dick Smith, and flew out of Sydney under the command of Captain Ken Nicholson. The Qantas Antarctic charters continued until early 1980 when they ceased in the aftermath of the Air New Zealand accident at Mount Erebus. The flights resumed on New Year's Eve 1994, with Qantas flying six flights that first season.

Despite its remote location and inhospitable environment, Antarctica is a region that continues to provide a wealth of scientific data to researchers on the ground and a sense of wonder to airborne tourists alike. And on closer examination, some of its data is impressive.

Covering fourteen million square kilometres Antarctica is near twice the size of Australia and accounts for 90 per cent of the world's fresh water in the form of ice. This ice covers more than 99 per cent of the continent with an average thickness of 2,000 metres and only the coastal rocky outcrops and rising mountain peaks escape the ice sheet. Its average elevation of 2,300 metres makes it the highest continent on earth, the coldest with a recorded temperature of -89.6C and the windiest, with gravity-assisted katabatic winds hurtling down the slopes at up to 320 km/h. The minimal amount of moisture received by the polar plateau compares to the driest deserts on earth. Antarctica is a unique place and while its mystery and majesty draws scientists and tourists, it also called for a range of additional considerations for aircraft venturing into the region.

The flight schedule was planned a year in advance and the crews that operated the service attended specialised briefings. In his role as Antarctic Charter Co-Ordinator, Captain Greg Fitzgerald oversaw the flights in a role that covered every imaginable aspect of flight operations. From navigation to airspace requirements, crew briefings to onboard camera equipment and the all-important meteorological updates - these were just some of the many strands that needed to be drawn together before the Boeing 747-400 ever left the ground.

The nature of the environment was unlike any other into which the airline operated. There were peaks reaching 16,000 feet, although the highest mountain in our potential area of operations was Mount Minto which towered at 13,600 feet. Consequently, the Lowest Safe Altitude (LSALT) for operations was a significant consideration.

Furthermore, throughout the flight GPS allowed a precise track to be flown, however, the heading reference of the aircraft would be switched from magnetic to true as the 747 passed 60 degrees South. Less technical, but equally vital, were a series of topographical 'strip maps' which added to the overall situational awareness of the crew.

Communications were primarily through datalink and Australian, New Zealand and the United States airspace all came into play. Additionally, contact was made with McMurdo Station approaching the scenic viewing area and Traffic Information Broadcasts by Aircraft (TIBA) are made on schedule over Antarctica.

As safety was the prime consideration, the importance of a positive hand-over-takeover procedure between pilots was reinforced to ensure that one pilot was always maintaining a positive watch over the aircraft. And while this may have seemed self-evident, such amazing scenery as the pilots would witness required positive cockpit discipline to avoid any lapse in monitoring the aircraft's flight path with reference to the instruments.

Well in advance of the day, the aircraft for the flight was identified and specifically tracked through the maintenance system to avoid any technical issues on the day. Additionally, the aircraft was required, before departure, to be fitted with a specially approved camera and in-flight audio equipment which will permit specialist commentary to the cabin on the day and footage to produce a DVD.

The day before our Antarctic charter was to fly from Melbourne, we gathered in Sydney. Captain Martin Buddery, who was commanding the flight, First Officer Andrew Packwood, Second Officer Mitch Clarke, and myself were joined by the Qantas meteorological and flight-planning briefing officers. Both the aircraft and Captain Fitzgerald were already in Melbourne and he participated in the briefing via a conference call.

The flights from Melbourne had three predetermined routes, each passing over Tasmania but each making landfall at Antarctica at a different point. From that point, the aircraft would leave the route and subsequently operate in a broader area over Antarctica. The meteorological forecast was particularly important as it aimed to identify the most suitable region for viewing based upon the predicted cloud cover and conditions. How this area was identified was both technically interesting and traditionally accurate.

Compiled in a 'T-36 hours' printed package, a wealth of information was available to the crew, supported by a face-to-face briefing by QMet. Opening with a plain English appreciation of the synoptic situation and a recommended route based upon those conditions, the package included Terminal Area Forecasts (TAF) and pictorial presentations outlining various analyses and forecasts including cloud cover, winds, and significant weather.

With the aircraft at the ready, the meteorological situation reviewed, and a provisional flight plan agreed upon, the meeting was concluded, and we made our way to Melbourne for the day that lay ahead.

The day began before 5 am for the crew. In Sydney, Flight Dispatch and QMET had already been busily gathering the latest data to relay to the crew as evidenced by the prompt that appeared on my iPad when it is brought to life. The flight plan and latest weather forecasts were available, and everything seemed in line with the detailed briefing of the day before.

The glow of iPads was the only illumination as the bus made its way to the airport. The latest briefing material had been uploaded as well as the flight plan which included an additional detail in its ATC flight strip - the maximum viewing time over Antarctica. By the time the crew was seated in the domestic terminal's briefing room - yes, this was a domestic service - all the information had been reviewed and the discussion fundamentally reinforced the anticipated plan and considered the critical differences of the Antarctic operation one more time.

The engineers called to advise that the Boeing 747-400 VH-OEG had been fuelled to its maximum capacity of just over 178 tonnes, given the current Specific Gravity (SG) of the fuel. They also confirmed that the aircraft had been fitted with the additional audio-visual equipment and the paperwork had been completed.

Aside from the digital flight plan, there was additional paperwork to be completed for the Australian Antarctic Division (AAD) in Hobart. AAD was the Government Department that approved Qantas to conduct these flights over Antarctica, based on environmental impact studies that Qantas supplied and logs that would be kept during actual flights. The Antarctic Flight Summary and Environment Log would be filled out in real-time beyond 60 degrees South latitude and submitted to AAD after the flight.

We then made our way down the hallway where Captain Buddery addressed the Cabin Crew for the flight. There was a tangible level of excitement among the crew who were a mix of senior flight attendants and relative newcomers but who all shared a common fascination with the flight ahead.

There was still well over an hour until departure and the gate lounge was full of excited passengers ranging from school students to a pair celebrating their ninetieth birthdays. Each with a name tag on their chest and vying for a photograph with the Penguin mascot, there was no mistaking that this was not your everyday service. Even with a comfortable margin of time until the Boeing pushed back, we were busy readying the aircraft inside and out. This included confirming the operation of the specially fitted entertainment system and that it was in working order throughout the cabin. Then, as the sun edged above the horizon in the east, the last door of the 747 was closed and all was ready for the journey southward.

At 406,000 kilograms, the aircraft was still more than 6,000 kg under its maximum take-off weight. Under Captain Buddery's hand, it lined up on Melbourne's Runway 34 and was given take-off clearance. With the clearance confirmed by the entire crew, the thrust levers were advanced and the four-engined giant began to accelerate. At 173 knots the Boeing is rotated, lifting its nose from the runway and began its climb into the morning sky.

The air was smooth as the four-hour sector to the ice began. There was extensive overcast below and Tasmania only peeked through a break in the cloud as the 747 passed overhead. There was a rare opportunity for me to mingle with the passengers and answer a constant stream of questions about the 747 and the flight. Interestingly, I had multiple questions for the young PhD students from the University of Melbourne.

Stationed by one of the aircraft doors, the scientists had set up a range of equipment to conduct experiments relating to cosmic radiation and the earth's magnetic field. And while they were impressed by their GPS's read-out of over 300 km/h during the take-off roll, it was one of their instruments that was particularly impressive to me - the 'Dip Circle'.

Measuring around 15cm in diameter, the brass ring possessed a dual face of glass with a needle inside. It resembled a large, see-through compass and was designed to measure the vertical component of a magnetic field - or 'dip'. Made in the 19th Century, this piece of scientific craftsmanship had journeyed to Antarctica before, by boat in 1910. It was appropriate that scientific research was on board the

Qantas aircraft as Australia's association with Antarctica dated back to 1886 when an Australian Antarctic Committee was founded.

Enroute, a phone patch had been organised for Captain Fitzgerald to interview Christine "Chris" MacMillan, the leader at Casey Station, which was broadcast through the cabin. In a fascinating exchange, Chris informed the passengers of the various aspects of life at an Antarctic Research Station. How the 120 crew was scaled back to just 30 in the winter months, the importance of working as a team and recreational activities which even included a dip into the icy waters on Australia Day.

With two hours remaining until we reached the Antarctic continent, we were busy with a range of duties. Critical fuel calculations and maximum viewing times were confirmed, contact was made with McMurdo station, an updated briefing was obtained from QMet, and the latest altimeter settings were gathered from various bases in Antarctica, with the most conservative being chosen for altimetry purposes when the aircraft descended. And that time was approaching.

Passing 60 degrees South the crew commenced their additional logs, ensured that the topographical strip maps were at hand and switched the 747's heading reference from Magnetic to True as the deviation between the two became too great nearing the South Pole.

The cloud cover slowly started to break up below and then 'Land Ho'. In the distance, jutting up were the jagged peaks of Antarctica. With altimetry, viewing time and critical scenarios double-checked, the aircraft began its descent to a Minimum Safe Altitude of 18,000 feet. McMurdo has advised us that the LC-130 aircraft that was inbound had returned to Christchurch due to a technical issue, making our 747 the only aircraft in the area. Even so, reports of our position were routinely made by datalink and broadcast on VHF radio.

Towering Mount Minto came into view and the sheer enormity of Antarctica became apparent. Landfall was made at Cape Adare and planned before a short westbound leg was flown, but it was apparent that the meteorological team was correct, and a cloud bank obscured the route. We turned back towards the Transantarctic Mountain Range, with the view made even more spectacular by the pristine air.

As I focused the lens beyond the instrument panel's glareshield, my camera captured towering mountain peaks, razor-edged ranges, and glaciers at every turn. Some of these were filled with reef-like lines of blue ice which formed when snow fell on a glacier and became compressed, squeezing out air bubbles and allowing the ice crystals to enlarge. Beyond the coast, the water was partially covered by pack-ice with mammoth mesa-like icebergs rising from the sea while their greater mass lurked below.

An 'ice tongue' extended out onto the water's surface where the glacier's momentum had carried it beyond the landmass. Nearby, a patch of brown clearing was the site where the first men, Norwegians, had spent a night in Antarctica in 1899. Their hut remained, barely visible from altitude, a silent witness to a bold age of exploration. With every turn, there was something new - either just off the wing or extending far past the focus of the human eye.

All the while, the expert commentary was provided through the cabin by Mike Craven, a scientist who had spent a significant time in the region. Fascinating facts, from the findings of 3,000-metre-deep ice cores to Patagonian dust and the formation of snowflakes. In the cabin, the excitement and chatter didn't cease. Fingers pointed and smiles beamed as one bucket list after another was kicked over. The seating arrangements were reorganised halfway through during the total viewing time of 3 hours and 40 minutes to share the vista.

On the flight deck, the view was also appreciated but we still attended to our duties with the required discipline and discussed where might be the next snowbound area to investigate. Logs were completed, broadcasts were made, and calculations were confirmed. The cycle of activity continued.

The passage of time was rapid over this timeless continent and soon it was time to depart. The intentions of our Qantas Boeing 747 were transmitted, and an airways clearance was sought. There was one last wave of farewell to Cape Adare before we climbed back into the flight levels and Qantas Flight 2907 set a northerly course and headed for home.

The sun set as Bass Strait slid beneath. Many of the passengers were now asleep with the return flight having been less dramatic than the scenery they had witnessed. However, by the time the aircraft had parked at the gate, their enthusiasm had returned and, one after another, they filed onto the flight deck. Smiling from ear-to-ear, some were as enchanted by the flight deck of the 'Queen of the Skies' as they were Antarctica. Without exception, the passengers were abuzz and although it had been a long day, we attended to them one by one and reflected the excitement that they expressed.

Astronaut Buzz Aldrin had a turn of phrase to describe the moon when he set foot on the surface in 1969. It captured the amazement of an expanse, untouched by man and almost overpowering in its enormity. It is a phrase that may well suit Antarctica and be uttered by those that have witnessed it from the skies – "Magnificent Desolation".

CHAPTER TWENTY-SEVEN
ALOHA AND GOODBYE.

I f one port in the network rivalled my fondness for San Francisco, it was Honolulu. It was a relatively short sector of nine hours by night to fly to Hawaii, while the return leg was a day sector, arriving home refreshed and with minimal jet lag. The flight home was spectacular because even though we crossed the Pacific regularly, it was usually by night, obscuring the ocean below with its amazing mix of blues and greens, atolls, and islands. And the morning arrival into Honolulu wasn't bad either.

The sun had risen an hour or two before it was time to descend, and the ritual of breakfast and briefing was completed among our three-pilot crew. The final miles of ocean transited waters populated by naval vessels of all sizes with a submarine sighting not being an uncommon occurrence.

The island of Oahu on which Honolulu is situated stood out from a distance, its deep greens, and grey rocky peaks reminiscent of the island in the famed "Jurassic Park" movie, which is not surprising as Oahu was the location for the film. Growing closer, the scene was even more picturesque as the crystal waters met the sand at the feet of the hills.

Our flight path rolled into a right-hand turn to align with the distant runway that ran parallel to the shoreline. To our right were clear blue waters and pure white clouds, to our left the emerald foliage which gradually gave way to lower-lying pastures.

Stage by stage the flaps were extended, and the landing gear was lowered. Steady, stable, and slowed down, the giant 747 sat with its nose slightly raised in a regal pose, its shoulders broad and unphased by the occasional ripple of turbulence - simply shrugging it off.

Ahead and to the left I sighted a break in the coast, a channel and it was unmistakable – it was Pearl Harbor. Having read so many books and viewed so many films about the attack on this harbour, it was incredible to think that I was about to pass this place of significance. Now, there were modern ships at the port but in the distance, I could see the USS Missouri at anchor, the "Mighty Mo." On those very decks, the surrender was signed in Tokyo Bay in 1945. The runway loomed large, with military aircraft to the left and right of the runways. To the left, an array of multi-engined airlift aircraft was parked and to the right, rows of the advanced fighter, the F-22 Raptor sought shade under shelters.

Our wheels kissed the burning asphalt and we had arrived once again. Having parked at the most distant parking bay, the walk to the Customs Hall took some time but soon enough we were hotel bound. Soon thereafter, I was swimming in the ocean waters adjacent to the hotel. That afternoon I hiked up Diamond Head where the view of Waikiki was laid out before me as I dripped in sweat. And each evening, the crowds would gather, but I would find a quiet place to call my own and watch the sun set. The Hawaiian sunsets were as beautiful as any I have witnessed – a glowing orange ball that turned the sky amber and silhouetted the sails of the yachts cruising the horizon.

I had visited Pearl Harbor previously and wandered among the museums and memorials, none more poignant than the grave of the USS Arizona. From the memorial one could look upon the submerged battleship, the resting place of more than 1,100 sailors and officers. Occasionally, a drop of oil would breach the surface, and these have become known as the "tears of the Arizona."

As was my way, on that same trip I had wanted to see this historic harbour from the air and fly through the same skies that had filled with fire in 1941. And this was not a flight to be flown in a modern trainer or helicopter, I wanted to be aloft in an aircraft of the era – a warbird. The aircraft was a single-engined T-6 SNJ trainer, painted in the markings of a Navy "tailhook" from the ship, the USS Saratoga.

First, we briefed the "mission," which was to be a simulated photographic reconnaissance flight that would circumnavigate the island via a list of significant waypoints from that fateful day. I was shown photographic images and short films, estimated casualties and damage to the fleet. All the while I was steadily appreciating the scope of the attack beyond the shores of Pearl Harbor. The airfields, the radar station, the diverted bombers, and the few allied fighters that were able to bravely offer resistance in the face of overwhelming numbers. The raw footage and cold statistics were sobering and struck with a deeper impact than any Hollywood blockbuster could ever hope to achieve. Then it was time to fly.

Parachute on and strapped in low and tight, I rehearsed the bailout drill from my position in the rear seat. Headset off, unstrap harness, lock canopy open and dive over the right-hand side of the cockpit, aiming for the wing's trailing edge. As I repeated the drill, I surveyed that everything about this aircraft exuded an air of safe passage and security, from the girder-like framework that enveloped me, to the sizeable North American rudder pedals in front.

The aeroplane came to life with a puff of exhaust smoke and a throaty roar of the Pratt and Whitney radial engine. The two propeller blades blurred into a lone spinning disc and the instruments ahead of me came to life.

Lined up on the centreline, the throttle was opened smoothly, and I sank reassuringly into my seat. Soon the tail rose and then the aircraft's shadow fell away, skipping past the last remaining wartime hangar of Barber's Field. We rolled gently to the left and set course to the north with the famous harbour out to our right.

History passed me by each minute. Wheeler Field where the P-40 Warhawks had been ablaze and the lesser-known coral runway, from where two young Army Air Corps pilots took off into a hostile sky. The site of the radar station that first detected the inbound Japanese armada of the skies and was mistaken for Boeing B-17 Flying Fortresses inbound from the mainland. Bellows Airfield and the beach where a midget submarine had been dragged onshore. As I wheeled to the left and right, I was struck by the reality that these were the same parcels of space through which the Japanese fighters and bombers had passed on the way to their targets.

We slipped between two jagged peaks to emerge with Waikiki in the distance on our left and Pearl Harbor straight ahead. Ford Island, with its runway and orange-and-white-striped control tower loomed large, as did the massive battleship Missouri, now at anchor and standing watch over the sunken USS Arizona. From my vantage point overhead, I pictured the white wake of the torpedoes threading towards "battleship row." The smell of burning oil and the rising funnels of black smoke. The noise must have been deafening on the land, sea and in the air.

By contrast, my skies were clear and blue, and the only sound was the rhythmic, reliable hum of the SNJ's engine. There was hardly a ripple in the air or on the water and the magic of flight was at its absolute best. The here-and-now was in stark contrast with history, and the outline of the sunken Arizona could still be seen through the clear waters as I passed overhead. This single image broke through my wistful pondering of flight and prevented me from being lost in the moment. Nor should I have been, as this was a site of solemn significance and deserved respect and remembrance.

The USS Missouri and Ford Island slipped from view behind the tailplane and our nose was once again pointed towards Barber's Field. I looked down at the water and waves off the wing tip as the nose rolled about the horizon to align with the runway. The wheels touched down and eventually, the blurred disc again became two stationary propeller blades. I slid the canopy back, with my harness and headset still in place, and a hint of oil fumes mingled with the salt air. I leaned my head back and all I could see was the blue sky, bordered by the framework of the 1940s cockpit. There were no visual cues of the present era as I looked into those historic skies above me. That very same piece of sky, but in such a vastly different time.

Those thoughts were still with me each time I arrived and departed Honolulu and the departure was as stunning as they come. We taxied out to a distant runway located on the water's edge. Along a narrow stretch, the taxiway was bordered by shallow, brilliant blue waters on either side. Lined up to take-off, Diamond Head could be seen dead ahead, just beyond the buildings of Waikiki.

No sooner were we airborne than a right turn was commenced with the 747's wingtip drawing an arc upon the ocean as a vessel passed just below us, its white wake in contrast with the blue. Wings levelled, the climb continued until Oahu was just a memory - until next time.

The hours always seemed to pass more quickly by day. The deeper blues of the ocean where a cavernous trench lay beneath and the light aquas where the sand shifted just below the surface. Random coral atolls formed shapes like hearts and daggers, while others still carried the scar of a wartime airstrip carved into their face. Past Howland Island where Amelia Earhart was bound for but never arrived. Was her Lockheed Electra on the ocean floor beneath my feet? Other small islands flitted by, forgotten other than for their bloody battles of World War Two.

Massive clouds brewed into even larger storms which by day were easily seen, avoided, and even admired for their power. We transited the airspace of Fiji before the Australian accent of Brisbane Centre filled our headsets.

Unlike the rest of the Pacific, Sydney was grey and overcast as we broke out from beneath the cloud base and touched down on runway 16 Right. The spectre of the COVID-19 pandemic had been growing in its inertia and as we parked the 747 that day, we all wondered what that may mean for our industry. Still, at that moment I could not conceive that I had just flown my final commercial service on the mighty Boeing 747.

PART FOUR
FAREWELL FROM THE FLIGHT DECK.

CHAPTER TWENTY-EIGHT
THE BEGINNING OF THE END.

The retirement of the Qantas Boeing 747-400 fleet was always planned to be a gradual, orderly process, having begun with the retirement of the first 400s, years earlier. A list had long been in circulation showing the proposed month that each of the remaining aircraft would leave the fleet until the book was finally closed on its long and honourable service with the airline. Of those still in service, the Rolls Royce engined aircraft would be the first to depart and gradually the GE-powered "Extended Range" variants would fade away with 2021 marked as the finale, marking an amazing half-century of service with the Flying Kangaroo for the 747.

The first Qantas 747-400, VH-OJA, the City of Canberra, had gone with much fanfare to be preserved at the Historical Aircraft Restoration Society (HARS) Museum, south of Sydney in March 2015. As the centrepiece of the museum's vast collection, its red fin greets visitors to Shellharbour Airport, where she continues to welcome passengers on board, even if only for a guided tour of her now-static airframe.

One by one, the 747s slipped quietly away, most bound for the "boneyard" storage facility at Victorville, California where they slowly waited in the dry desert air to be scrapped. Unwanted after a life of loyal service. Some were to be found elsewhere awaiting a similar fate, while the original "Wunala" (VH-OJB), which had borne the brilliant red Aboriginal artwork, made one final hop across to the Mojave Air and Space Port, also in California. Wearing a traditional Qantas scheme, sans the Flying Kangaroo and other markings, OJB bore the US registration of N954JM scrappily spray-painted on her nose gear door for the short ferry flight.

A happier fate met VH-OJU in 2019 when it escaped the scrapper's axe after twenty years of service and the equivalent of one hundred return trips to the moon in the miles that it had covered. "Lord Howe Island", as it was named, was destined to become an engine testbed for Rolls Royce where it would provide vital data for the next generation of jet engines. Appropriately, it would bear the new US registration of N747RR.

The ERs were to follow the Rolls Royce aircraft in an equally orderly fashion with a celebration of fifty years of the Qantas 747 to farewell the final aircraft in March 2021. And then the pandemic gripped the world and threw air travel into absolute disarray. Aircraft now sat idle in storage at their home ports, not some distant boneyard. Sealed up with tape and their engine intakes covered, the airports of the world had fallen all but silent. The fate of the airline's final 747s was unknown and Kirrily and I were caught in the centre of the uncertainty.

When Ansett had collapsed, I'd not been aware that my final flight was the end of the road, and that feeling came across me once again. Was that sun-drenched departure from Honolulu the last time that I would feel the 747 rise into the air? Was it the end of my airline career?

Kirrily and I each received letters from the airline standing us down from duty for the foreseeable future. The absence of any timeframe was the most difficult element to grasp. As pilots, we were trained to assimilate all the available information, formulate a strategy and mitigate risk. The problem was that there was no information – nobody knew what COVID-19 meant for the world in April of 2020. Maybe it would last six months – maybe longer?

There was a slight sense of Déjà vu in that I was made redundant during the Ansett collapse – but that was different. That was the end of an individual airline and passenger demand was still strong. This was a global crisis. Still, this time I was better prepared with secondary employment as a writer and consultant, while Kirrily had rolled up her sleeves and was employed at the local hospital. We employed our skillset as pilots to formulate a strategy; it was just that the strategy did not involve flying for an airline.

Despite the absence of work with Qantas, Kirrily and I had been more fortunate than most. As we were both flying the 747, there had been opportunities to share the flight deck. Her parents had kindly cared for our kids, allowing us to see in New Year's Eve by the waterfront in San Francisco and land upon a crystal-clear lake that was fed by a glacier near Vancouver. There were so many cherished memories of people, places and unique experiences that had been afforded to us through our time on the 747. We had no complaints.

I had been fortunate across my entire career. I had over 20,000 hours in the air flying a range of aircraft, from biplanes to Boeings. I had flown for three airlines and held a command, after a career flying smaller aircraft that I thoroughly enjoyed. I had seen the magnificent desolation

of Antarctica at close range, and Mount Everest in the distance. I had retraced my father's footsteps in Tokyo and shared tea with Battle of Britain veterans in England. I had eaten sea urchins in Paris. And even though I had only flown a single Santiago service, the sight of that city surrounded by the snow-capped Andes mountains was not one that I would soon forget. So, if that flight from Hawaii was my last sector, what a wonderful final memory that would be.

Rather than sit and wait, I dedicated myself to other work. I was engaged by the Royal Australian Air Force to author a book on the Korean War, a conflict in which my father flew and a subject close to my heart. And there were other writing projects and volunteer work to keep me occupied as the world entered even darker times as the global death toll rose.

Kirrily and I both felt fortunate to have our family and fresh air in the most wonderful nation on earth – in our humble opinion. The future was uncertain, but we remained positive and hopeful and were thankful that we were healthy as terrible images from around the globe flashed across our screen. We took strength from being a close-knit family and were open with our children about what was going on and what it potentially meant for our careers. Not with a sense of dread but with a pragmatic view to the future and the consideration that a new chapter may lie ahead.

We had both hoped to see the 747 through to retirement and then train upon another aircraft type. It had only been another year away when the pandemic intervened, and we had looked forward to saying farewell to an aircraft that had forged an incredible aviation legacy – but that was not to be.

By May, the rumours were already circulating that 747 was to be retired earlier than scheduled and the remaining ERs were being readied to fly to the boneyards in the coming months. There would be no fanfare, no celebration of service, no landmark moment. Like their Rolls Royce sisters, they would one by one slip into one last night over the Pacific before being laid to rest in the desert sun and the word on the street was that would happen soon. The 747 had blazed a trail but now it would fade into history. It was apparent that the era had ended without a final curtain call.

And then my phone rang.

It was Captain Georgina Sutton, the Manager of Base Operations in Sydney and she posed a confidential, hypothetical scenario? If the final Boeing 747-400 was to depart the country, would I like to be involved? Nothing was certain. Nothing was public. She was just seeking an expression of interest. My interest was piqued, and my answer was, "Yes"! Georgina closed with the comment that if it went ahead, I would be required to return to the simulator to regain my currency on the aeroplane and someone would be in touch if that was to happen.

When the call came, it was Captain Marty Gardiner, a pilot and friend that I'd known from the 1980s at the Royal Aero Club of NSW. Marty was one of the captains that had been tasked with keeping crews current on the 747 to complete the final flights. He was also rostered to take VH-OEE to Mojave in June and this seemed to confirm that the last 747s were departing in sequence, bound for the Mojave Desert via Los Angeles.

On the last day of May, I was back in the 747 simulator for a session alongside another pilot bound for Mojave. I doubt that I had ever been happier to be strapped into the heaving box on its hydraulic legs and it was great to feel connected with the aircraft and the airline once again. When the session was completed, it was confirmed that the last 747 was scheduled to depart on June 30th and the aircraft would be VH-OEJ, "Wunala".

At this stage, the flight was still confidential as the ability for the crew to return from the USA, given the current state of the pandemic, was a day-to-day proposition. No certainty could be attached to a date, or even the flight taking place and it was better for the moment to fly beneath the media's radar.

I made an exception and told one other 747 pilot the tentative plan in secrecy – that pilot was Kirrily.

CHAPTER TWENTY-NINE
THE LAST GOODBYES.

There was one interesting aspect to the veil of secrecy – the internet. My feed was filled with theories about when the last aircraft was really departing, where it was really going and who had really bought the airframe and engines. The truth was I had a tentative understanding of the where and the when and the rumours were nearly all incorrect. As for who was buying the aircraft, that would be a confidential matter at a corporate level way above my pay grade. However, someone always knew someone, whose brother said something about the final 747's fate. I just bit my lip and kept my word as still so much could have changed. And it did.

The proposed departure date was moved from June 30th to July 22nd, but for a very good reason – the 747 was to be farewelled in the best style possible given the restrictions imposed by the pandemic. The plan was drafted to hold three farewell flights, with one each flying from Sydney, Brisbane, and Melbourne, respectively. However, with the tenuous state of Victoria's borders and public health situation, the first casualty was the Melbourne flight, causing it to be moved to Canberra. There was more news forthcoming regarding the farewell with the official announcement of our departure date on July 22nd and thankfully, I no longer had to keep those cards so close to my chest.

Announced early in July, with the bottom line of all airlines impacted, the "joy flights" were brought to life through a skeleton staff being stood up from their relative hibernation to address every issue from media relations, to engineering, flight planning, crewing, and so much more. Even assigning the flight number of QF747 presented a significant challenge within the airline's IT systems, but it soon became apparent that the flights meant a great deal to the Qantas family as well as the staff that came together to make the event happen.

A lottery system was devised to allow some of that family to gain a seat on their airline's final 747 flights, while other seats were sold online to offset some of the costs involved and raise funds for two aviation museums. Tickets were $400 for Economy Class and $747 for Business Class. The demand far outweighed availability, and the tickets sold in minutes. In a fortunate twist of fate, Kirrily won a ticket in the staff lottery, and I was so happy for her. She had a long association with the 747 beyond her years at Qantas as her father, Barrie, had flown the 747 "Classic" models for the airline. No doubt, more flights could have been sold out, but the timeframe was already in place for OEJ to depart on July 22nd and the clock was ticking.

For the first flight, the Sydney skies were forecast to be grey and damp, but the Queen of the Skies would not be denied. Under blue skies and with fair winds at their backs, people made their way to Sydney Airport where the 747 was in its final stages of preparation.

From the moment that Kirrily and I entered the terminal, there was a throb among those that had gathered. Antique Qantas travel bags, old boarding passes and uniforms of yesterday were there to be seen. Past Qantas pilots, aviation enthusiasts and families waited for the boarding call that would signal the move to Boeing 747-400, VH-OEJ. Kirrily and I mingled with passengers and answered questions, helping more than one person capture that final shot with the 747 as the backdrop.

Pushed back, clear of the tug and free to taxi under her own power, the OEJ, "Wunala," was saluted by a pair of fire tenders before it took to the skies. Those on board were treated to a unique experience in an aircraft the size of the 747 to the soundtrack of popping champagne corks. Tracking as far north as the Central Coast, west to Narellan and south to the National Park, flypasts of both Sydney Harbour and the airport were undoubtedly the highlight for many. Aside from the significance of the day, the low density of air traffic due to the pandemic undoubtedly assisted with such generous airways clearances around the city. For well over an hour those passengers enjoyed the experience of a lifetime, while for many of the crew it was the end of a personal journey.

The festivities continued once the giant had been towed into the Qantas Hangar 96. Stories were exchanged, food was consumed, and surplus Qantas cabin items were sold off to raise money for charity. The crew posed for photos as they showed passengers through the flight deck before more images were captured by the engine intakes.

Outside, staff queued for their chance for one last meeting with the 747. And while OEJ was at rest, it was only catching its breath after this short sprint. There were still two more joy flights to complete before her final journey. Next, she was to travel to Brisbane and then the final joy flight would originate in the nation's capital, Canberra.

Living only a couple of hours from Canberra, Kirrily and I volunteered to drive south to assist in any way we could. We had seen the excitement of the Sydney flight first-hand and the enthusiasm of passengers to discuss the 747 with crew members. On another brilliant day, "Wunala" treated passengers to views of Parliament House, Lake Burley Griffin and the Snowy Mountains which were capped in winter snow.

Captain Greg Fitzgerald and his wife were also in Canberra that day, volunteering to assist and answer questions. Greg was one of the captains that interviewed me for my job at Qantas and had also been behind the Antarctic charters. More importantly, he had introduced me to an excellent restaurant in Tokyo. Now we were both among the crew for the 747 final farewell to the United States, a flight that would also likely mark Greg's retirement. A flight that was only days away.

Just as Kirrily and I had witnessed in Sydney, the terminal was abuzz both before and after the flight, passengers proudly displayed the mementos of the flight that came with the ticket, from bags and baseball caps to safety cards, stickers, and certificates. It was a wonderful experience to be a part of, although when "Wunala" departed Canberra for Sydney everyone, including Kirrily and I, realised that the end was nigh. Just, one more familiar Pacific crossing before a short hop to the Mojave Desert where those mighty engines would finally fall silent.

However, there was still one final act to play out before the 747 slipped into the long goodnight.

CHAPTER THIRTY
PLANNING AND PREPARATION.

B efore the announcement of the flight was official, the crew had been selected and we had all been hard at work. The crew comprised of Sharelle Quinn, the first female Qantas Captain, and the airline's most senior 747 Captain Ewen Cameron, who would fly the initial departure. Also, onboard would be Captains Owen Weaver and Greg Fitzgerald, First Officer Quin Ledden, and a truly fortunate, me. Together, we had over 124,000 hours of flight experience, including more than 78,000 hours on the 747.

Despite the level of experience, planning, preparation, and training remained pivotal to the success of the flight and had found the crew spending hours in the simulator to regain currency and to rehearse for the unique nature of the flight. Central to the departure were three key elements – a flypast of Sydney Harbour, a salute to the record-breaking and first 747-400, VH-OJA which was now in residence at the HARS Museum, and 'sky art' in the form of the Qantas kangaroo.

The centrepiece of the departure was set to be the sky art kangaroo, yet when Captain Weaver first conceived the idea, he wasn't even sure if it was possible. In the first instance, he overlaid the outline in Google Earth Pro and generated a series of waypoints. As these were expressed in decimal points, all seventy-five had to be converted into latitudes and longitudes. Scaling the sky art was the next challenge. Turns had to be of a radius within the capability of the heavily-laden 747 and of a size and location to be seen by the flight tracking 'apps' without dropping out of ADS-B coverage.

While the harbour flypast and the salute to OJA had been part of the official announcement, the sky art remained a closely guarded secret. For the kangaroo to be drawn, certain parameters beyond our control had to be met, notably an absence of turbulence and a specific limit on the prevailing wind velocity. Secrecy was not maintained to keep the media out of the loop, but the reality was that unless the conditions were suitable and safe, the kangaroo would not be drawn. Announcing the concept in advance, creating excitement and then being unable to execute would have been disappointing for all parties. There were also limiting weather conditions for the two flypasts but, unlike the sky art, if low cloud, wind, or rain prevented their execution, the reason would be evident to those gathered on the ground.

Captain Weaver had flown a series of secretive simulator sessions with Captain Marty Gardiner in a range of configurations to determine the feasibility of drawing the kangaroo. Finally, remaining below 20,000 feet so that flaps could be extended and then utilising Flaps 20 and the autopilot, all turns within the 'roo could be safely flown.

The entire exercise had to be built upon a foundation of safety and, to that end, each component was planned, trained, and executed according to a safety plan that had gained approval from the Civil Aviation Safety Authority (CASA). Far from simply conceiving a route, myriad elements had to also be addressed.

Unlike the farewell flights, OEJ would be operating at a significantly heavier weight, and flight margins, particularly in terms of airspeed, needed to be considered. The crew would attend the event before departure and, with substantial flight time, potential fatigue issues needed to be addressed and satisfied. This was mitigated by carrying a "heavy crew" of six pilots –two more than the number legally required.

Security considerations and customs clearance at the Qantas hangar, rather than the international terminal had to be organised. Calculating the weight and balance of the aircraft and loading it accordingly, with a cargo that included several family pets bound for the USA. The list went on.

Captain Weaver drew together teams from all areas within the airline. Qantas Air Traffic Management was responsible for organising the complex airways clearances, as well as designing the Temporary Restricted Area (TRA) that was needed to safely overfly the HARS Museum outside controlled airspace. The navigation team were tasked with tailoring the existing flight planning system to incorporate the many complex waypoints involved in drawing the sky art and calculating the fuel requirements.

Catering was needed to provide meals for the crew, and the refuellers had to load the aircraft to maximum limits without fuel overflowing through the surge tanks. The Airports Team and Sydney Airports Corporation Limited (SACL) had to confirm the pavement strength was sufficient in the alleyway from the hangar where OEJ would taxi at a weight of 368,000 kg.

The QMET section consistently provided weather and upper wind forecasts, as the sky art and flypasts were particularly weather-dependent. Furthermore, they were continually organising weather forecasts for Mojave, an airport for which such reports were not normally provided.

The engineering team had to prepare the aircraft for international flying once again, ground testing the autopilot for auto-land capability, and configuring the cabin for its ultimate state when it finally parked in the boneyard, among other tasks.

An event was planned before departure to bring together as many members of the Qantas family as COVID restrictions would permit. Organising the event to be held in Qantas Hangar 96 fell on the shoulders of the Qantas Events Team, while the associated media was managed by the Communications Department. With the approval and cooperation of the Royal Australian Air Force, airspace was made available off the east coast that provided the elements needed to have the sky art "seen" around the world.

The role of the airline cannot be understated. Qantas was in the grips of a pandemic, its aircraft grounded and the company was haemorrhaging funds. Still, it recognised the 747 as the peoples' aeroplane and one that had been intertwined with Qantas history for 49 years. The 747 had opened the world to Australians on a scale they had never known, through memories of amazing holidays and emotional family reunions. If there was a poignant moment in an Australian life beyond her shores, the chance was great that the 747 had made that possible. With this in mind, Qantas wanted to share the moment with the people, albeit with strict COVID-19 protocols in place.

The entire process was a textbook example, not only of planning but interoperability. If at any stage, communication or co-operation had broken down, the 747 could not have left on its final journey with a farewell to remember. And while the planners planned, the pilots prepared. Emails carried charts and data relating to the flights, both to Los Angeles and the short sector to Mojave. Briefing notes for the latter were provided by crews, including Captain Weaver, who had taken previous 747s to the boneyard. How each sequence would be flown, the configuration of the aircraft for each manoeuvre, the radio frequencies, the limits of airspace and airspeed restrictions were a portion of the considerations that were discussed.

With a plan in place, simulator sessions were flown to rehearse the various sequences. These provided more than an opportunity to "fly" and "see" the various components of the flights, it allowed the recording of timings and the amount of fuel consumed which were both essential factors in achieving the desired outcome. Captain Ewen Cameron and Captain Fitzgerald flew the LAX to Mojave sector a number of times to prepare for the descent and the visual approach into Mojave with the airspace of Edwards Air Force Base nearby.

As the day approached, I organised my charts and notes into a dedicated folder in the order they would take place. I had magnified and printed out sections of the charts where airspace was nearby, highlighting geographic features and recording radio frequencies in the margins. Other information included the flap setting, speed, and sequence for every stage of the flypasts and sky art.

The night before, I packed my bag and readied my uniform. And just as I had on that first 747 flight nearly twenty years before, I slipped my dad's Qantas Empire Airways wings into the pocket of my shirt. He was going to make this trip with me as well.

CHAPTER THIRTY-ONE
A Day To Remember.

As always, I was running early. Kirrily and I drove to the airport and made our way to Hangar 96 where "Wunala" was already parked, her tailing remaining outside the hangar entrance. Within the hangar, trestles carried food and drinks, decommissioned galley carts and trays of glasses were up for sale and rows of large images documented the history of the Boeing 747 in Qantas colours. The stage was set and now the guests just had to arrive.

Soon members of the Qantas family and special guests began to fill the hangar. Cabin Crew, engineers, ground staff and pilots of all eras filed in, some wearing their uniform and others wearing those of bygone times. One of those in his old uniform was Captain Dick Hodder – the past student of my father and the captain on my first 747 familiarisation flight to Cairns. The pandemic had limited how many could share the day, but the atmosphere was already beginning to bubble.

As those gathered mingled, the crew were occupied with various tasks. Owen and Greg were concealed on the flight deck, meticulously loading the 75 waypoints into the FMC that would craft the kangaroo sky art. The task had proven too much for the computing capacity of the system to be automatically uploaded. When that was completed, we were shepherded into an office to complete our security checks and customs clearance. Our bags were sealed, and I filed the paperwork in my flight bag.

As a crew, we had been in constant contact in the lead up to the flight, even so, when the day arrived a thorough briefing was required to confirm what was required in the day ahead. The best news was that the weather briefing indicated that conditions would be perfect both for the flypasts and the sky art. Even at this stage, knowledge of the plan to draw the kangaroo was very limited.

I rejoined Kirrily and we made our way over to "Wunala" where everyone was invited to ink their name and a short message on the belly of the aircraft. Kirrily paid tribute to her dad and his time flying the 747 and I wrote, "One more time with feeling" which partially conveyed my true sentiment of, "We're nearly there. Let's get this done smoothly, Wunala". Sharelle, Ewen, Greg and Quin all took their turn with the marker pen, media cameras eagerly filming over their shoulder.

The formalities were beginning soon, so we met with the Qantas CEO, Alan Joyce, and shared our thoughts about the flight ahead. Again, the cameras hovered, and we were fanned out either side of the boss and captured on film in a group shot. Over to one side, Kirrily was being interviewed and filmed.

Captain Mike Galvin was the Master of Ceremonies and conducted the event that included Aboriginal Elders performing "Welcome to Country", traditional music and laying of their hands upon the flanks of Wunala. First Officer Geoff Cowell recited a poem that he had written about the "Queen of the Skies" and the CEO spoke of the 747's amazing and pivotal role with Qantas. As a crew we stood together to one side, taking in the moment but I must confess that I found it difficult not to be running through the flight sequence in my head.

When the proceedings concluded, we knew that it was time to move. We had been given a short lesson on boarding the aircraft by media relations and we were to proceed two at a time, stop at the base of the stairs and wave and then move up the stairs. That was the trigger for the next pair to walk towards the stairs. Sharelle and Ewen led off, then Quin and me and finally Owen and Greg.

As instructed and evenly spaced, we turned back and waved. I realised that I was the only one not waving their hat and soon rectified that, although I was rather relieved not to have tripped up the stairs thus far. As we looked back, there was a small sea of red Qantas 747 flags waving and a few tears being shed – Kirrily included. At that point, Channel Ten thought it was an opportune time to grab a few words from the female pilot with tears in her eyes. Kirrily obliged with style.

The thump of the door closing behind us signalled that the business end of the day was about to begin. A large yellow note sat front and centre on the instrument panel. "FMC Route fully loaded. DO NOT TURN OFF IRSs". It was either Owen or Greg's handiwork reminding one and all not to interfere with the 75 kangaroo waypoints that had been manually and meticulously loaded by them over about 45 minutes.

Sharelle strapped into the left seat with Ewen in the right. Checklists were read and completed, and we waited for the signal that the push back out of the hangar was to begin. The call came from the ground crew and the beacon was selected on and the brakes released. As we slowly pushed back into the alleyway, the crowd continued to wave, possibly with even more energy. It was obvious what this aircraft meant to people, and I felt privileged to be on the flight deck and thankful for the opportunity to farewell the 747 in the proper fashion.

At the end of the alley, we started the four GE engines and were disconnected from the tug. In every direction, personnel had gathered on the tarmac and were waving. We gained taxi clearance from the Surface Movement Controller (SMC) and Sharelle slowly started Wunala on her journey under the callsign of "Qantas 7474".

The taxi route was an extended tour, heading south to where the runways crossed at which point, we were greeted by a water salute from the fire services. The ribbon of water arced towards us, and helicopters hovered overhead as we edged our way towards Shep's Mound near the base of the control tower. Shep's Mound was a known location for aircraft photographers that in recent years had been landscaped and equipped for that very role. We received clearance and Wunala came to a halt in front of the massive crowd both on the mound and lining the cyclone fence that bordered the airport. Australian flags were waving, and the western winter sun glinted off camera lenses and lit up the faces of those that had come to say goodbye to the "Queen of the Skies".

A little further on we were cleared to cross Runway 16 Right and head north to the runway's end. More cameras were atop tripods on the grass verge beside the runway, escorted by airport security vehicles with their flashing amber lights.

With the lap of honour completed, we all took a few deep breaths and confirmed that the checklists had been completed and Wunala was indeed ready for flight. She was and we were given clearance to line up and wait and advised that five helicopters were operating above the airfield that were responsible for remaining clear of our departure.

Then the clearance was given, "Qantas 7474 for the last time, your assigned heading is 155, Runway 16 Right, you're cleared for take-off."

On the flight deck, take-off clearance was confirmed and Sharelle moved the thrust levers forward, engines stabilised, she pushed the TO/GA buttons, the engines responded and Wunala began to slowly accelerate.

CHAPTER THIRTY-TWO
ONE MORE TIME
WITH FEELING.

"Thrust Set" Ewen called as every set of eyes on the flight deck scanned the engine instruments.

"Eighty knots"

"Checked" Sharelle acknowledged.

"V1"

That long pause that I knew so well.

"Rotate"

On this call, Sharelle eased the nose of Wunala skyward.

"Positive Rate" We were clear of the ground and climbing.

"Gear Up," Sharelle called for the landing gear to be retracted and we were underway.

At 1,000 Sharelle steered Wunala into a right-hand turn. The waters of Botany Bay were below where 250 years ago Captain Cook had anchored the HMS Endeavour, a vessel capable of a speed of 8 knots as it crossed the oceans. Tonight, we would bridge the Pacific at 500 knots. The right turn eventually brought us back to fly an easterly heading above Runway 07 at 1,500 feet. Kirrily was down there somewhere.

"Still the best-looking aeroplane in the sky." the controller commented across the frequency.

The flaps remained extended at "Flaps 10" allowing us to fly slow enough to offer those on the ground the best view and to maintain a reasonable radius of turn as we manoeuvred. Similarly, the autopilot remained engaged to allow the greatest margins of safety and permit the aircraft to be visually navigated with our eyes "outside" the flight deck, rather than being "head down".

From the airport we tracked to the iconic Bondi Beach, then after a left turn over the coastal waters, we lined up on North Head, gently waving the wings at the Qantas gathering as we entered the harbour towards Rose Bay where the Qantas "Empire" flying boats had once come and gone. The navigation display was marked with multiple helicopters on either side of our flight route and all eyes were peeled for any itinerant traffic.

And then the Opera House and Harbour Bridge loomed ahead, and those same helicopters positioned for their camera crews to catch the classic shot. Another wave of the wings was made to more of the Qantas family on the steps of the Opera House.

At 1,500 feet the flags atop the bridge were a sight to see as we passed by and headed west along the Parramatta River. As we reversed our direction to head back to the harbour, the place of my birth was in view and for a moment it seemed a little surreal. Another pass of Sydney Harbour and then we were bound to salute, VH-OJA.

Clear of the coast we turned right and on passing Cronulla planned to climb to 3,000 feet, raise the flaps to "Flaps 1" and accelerate to 260 knots with a clearance to do so by air traffic control. As we were about to request that clearance, ATC then transmitted a parting message.

"Qantas 7474, on behalf of all here at Sydney Air Traffic Control… It's been our pleasure to guide you through the skies safely and taking the Queen of the Skies through our airspace over the last decades."

He continued, "…as we all suffer through this COVID crisis, on behalf of Australian people across the country, many of whom have flown with you, it has been an uplifting experience to once again see Qantas raising the spirit of Australia with the flying kangaroo. God speed."

It was the most moving radio transmission that I'd ever heard.

Caught off guard by such a call, Ewen sincerely replied, "Mate. Thanks very much, we're all tearing up, up here."

We had to focus on the task and gain our clearance to climb, but moments like these made us realise just how special this day was.

Along the coast towards Wollongong, we left controlled airspace and eased back down to 1,500 feet to overfly Shellharbour Airport, HARS and VH-OJA. I was making the necessary inbound calls from the overflight when a well-wishing call from VH-OJA entered the flight deck. It was a significant moment. The first Qantas 747-400 bidding farewell to the final Qantas 747-400.

As Sharelle guided Wunala overhead the airport and into a left horseshoe to depart, the crowd could be seen below, surrounding OJA. I transmitted our request to re-enter controlled airspace and with the clearance granted, we left the "steel city" behind and began our climb to Flight Level 290 where we levelled off and all took a deep breath. Two of the three pivotal manoeuvres had been flown, now it was time to consider the sky art.

The crew briefed what was to be done. Speed management, flap extension and retraction, high altitude manoeuvring considerations such as bank angles and thrust. We also briefed the recovery from an incipient stall recovery – nothing was to be left to chance. A final assessment of the conditions and wind velocity were made, and we were clear to draw the 'roo.

I sent an ACARS message through to Qantas Sydney to inform them that the sky art would take place, cancelling months of secrecy and permitting the event to be released to the media.

The kangaroo was loaded into the FMC for the autopilot to follow and the process began. Different elements of the kangaroo called for different speeds, altitudes, and flap configurations. Each had been flown in the simulator and a checklist outlined what was needed for each phase. Long relatively straight sections such as the back could be flown higher and faster, whereas tight turns at the tip of the tail were flown lower and slower with the flaps extended to "20". The tip of the tail and the head contained the most critical turns.

From our easterly heading, our initial turn was back towards the coast to craft the back of the leg. (I was later told that certain folks in the United States thought we were returning to Sydney with a problem and so they went to bed). For the next ninety minutes, the 747 was carefully guided to craft a kangaroo in the sky that extended roughly 200 miles from its toe to tail. When it was completed, we had no way of knowing how it had translated on the various flight tracking apps until an ACARS message from Sydney arrived.

WELL DONE QF7474,

SKYART LOOKS AS PER PLANNED.

QF KANGAROO DRAWN BY THE QUEEN OF THE SKIES.

A NICE TRIBUTE ON BEHALF OF ALL THE PRECEDING MODELS OF THE 747.

FAREWELL 747 FROM ALL AT MAINTENANCE WATCH.

ACARS END

This indicated that the brainchild of Owen Weaver and all the hard work had paid off. The third event had been completed, so the crew resumed Pacific crossing mode and scheduled rest breaks, gathered weather reports, monitored fuel and engines. It seemed like any other night, but to be honest, it wasn't. There was no particular enthusiasm to take a rest break like there normally would be and when Quin and I were on watch, our meals were brought to the flight deck by two captains, Ewen and Greg. All the while, Owen's mascot, a kangaroo holding Australian and United States' flags sat atop the instrument panel. My kids had sent Bert, a small toy brown dog along for the ride. Bert had also travelled with me when I had flown solo around Australia in a light aircraft to raise funds for the Royal Flying Doctor Service – he was a well-travelled canine.

When I took my break, I wandered back through every inch of the cabin, nose to tail, upper deck, and my old crew rest. I filmed as I walked through row upon row of empty seats. The feeling had an eerie edge to it and reminded me that this truly was the last hop for Wunala. I returned to the crew rest, laid down and closed my eyes.

As always, the sun had returned as we descended over the Pacific towards Los Angeles. Santa Catalina Island, Runway 25 Left, it was all familiar but not taken for granted and briefed by the crew accordingly. Sharelle had not yet decided whether she would retire but we were all aware that this may be her final landing as the haze began to clear and the runway appeared ahead.

The multi-lane highways and residential areas gave way to industrial lots and finally the airport perimeter. Sharelle closed the thrust levers, and the wheels kissed the ground. Quin called "Speedbrake up"! Sharelle raised the reversers to the idle detent, and we had arrived at LAX.

We taxied clear of the runways to the Qantas facility, slowing to a halt before shutting the engines down. Outside, people had gathered on the roadway, some waving Australian flags as a team of Qantas ground staff came to meet the aircraft.

First on board was the Qantas LAX Airport Manager, Jaclyn Kinnane. I had known Jaclyn since she was a baby as her mother had been a Flight Nurse when my father flew the Air Ambulance, now she was running the show on the other side of the Pacific. Instinct was to give her a hug but the reality of face masks and COVID meant otherwise as the U.S. was being wracked by the pandemic in a way that Australia had yet to experience. This was reinforced as we proceeded through the customs hall where people in full protective equipment and plexiglass barriers were the norms.

In the minibus bound for the accommodation, our phones started to buzz wildly – particularly Owen Weaver's. Emails, texts, and messages were bombarding our devices with kangaroo sky art being the centre of attention. As we had transited the Pacific by night, the image of the kangaroo drawn off the Australian coast had gone viral across the internet and was being covered by major media outlets around the world.

The overwhelming feeling was one of relief, that the plan had been safely executed. All indications were that the farewell had been met with an overwhelming response. Perhaps the air traffic controller was right. Amid a pandemic, Wunala had given people a chance to forget the grim statistics and the uncertainty of the time that oozed from the media. The 747 had bumped the misery from the headlines and given people a reason to look up.

CHAPTER THIRTY-THREE
THE FINAL HOP.

Manhattan Beach is a nice part of Los Angeles, but we were effectively confined to quarters due to the pandemic. Other than a socially distanced debrief of the flight, we were in isolation in our rooms, other than to venture to Ralph's grocery store to purchase food and supplies. The walk to the Ralph's was an education as the Los Angeles I knew was now effectively a ghost town, other than the occasional jogger or an open food store.

Our rooms were split level, comfortable and with a small kitchen but it still seemed strange being alone within four walls after sharing the confines of a flight deck for so many hours. Still, I wasn't complaining.

The farewell flight had been an experience to rate among the most significant in my airline career and should the pandemic have ended my career; it would be a finale that would be difficult to beat. However, there was one short sector left to complete – from LAX to the Mojave Air and Space Port which would be Wunala's final resting place.

I kept busy in the days between flights "Face-timing" the family and diarising our flight from Sydney. I had also taken several photos that I was editing and sending through to Qantas media. I had also kept much of the paperwork for the flight that would normally be thrown out, knowing that when it came to writing any magazine articles, or even a book, these documents would be a tremendous resource.

173

Soon the emphasis shifted back to the task ahead and we readied for the final flight to Mojave. The weather forecast was clear for the 20-minute flight, and we reviewed the flight plan and fuel order as the minibus returned us to LAX. Captain Ewen Cameron would fly in command with Captain Greg Fitzgerald alongside him in a fitting end to their substantial Qantas careers. Both pilots had rehearsed the sector in the simulator numerous times, aware of the nearby terrain and the airspace of the famous Edwards AFB facility and other sensitive facilities.

When we arrived, we were greeted by Jaclyn and an amazing send-off. An old-style Aussie barbeque of sausages, bacon, and eggs was being served. Two dedicated 747 cakes were cut to a backdrop of Qantas banners and a small garden with a pedal car bearing the flying kangaroo mounted atop a pole. There was even a landing gear door carrying the markings of "OJM" on display and two staff had dressed in kangaroo and koala suits, respectively. Food was consumed and stories shared before a rendition of 'I Still Call Australia Home' was sung by the staff in what was a very moving moment. I looked around and realised that the Qantas family was as strong as it could ever be, even in the face of challenging times.

Well-fed we filed into the engineering office, where the last Technical Log entry from the engineer read:

FINISHED WITH THE ENGINES FOR THE LAST TIME. FAREWELL.

In turn, it was signed by Ewen and Greg with the notation.

HAPPY LANDINGS FOR EVERMORE.

Outside a crowd had gathered on the apron, with a ring of police vehicles nearby. On boarding, I fitted my high visibility vest and a face mask and descended the steps to perform the final "walkaround" inspection. It was a day of "finals."

I took my time, taking in the enormity of this mighty Boeing. Checking here, looking there. The massive bogies, the ever-reliable engines, and the beautiful sweep of those wings. Joe Sutter's design had certainly stood the test of time.

On the flight deck, the final checks were completed before the engines were started and we taxied for one last take-off, this time at a weight of only 228,000 kg. Water cannons again said goodbye as hundreds of Qantas staff and other airport workers lined the taxiway, and I thought how clean Wunala must be after the number of water salutes she had received in recent times.

Emergency vehicles ahead and on our flanks escorted us to the runway's end, lights flashing red, blue, and amber. We lined up on the runway and air traffic control cleared us with, "QF7474 Heavy Runway 25 Right, for the very last time, cleared for take-off".

Beneath Ewen's hands, the thrust levers advanced as helicopters above filmed and the people below waved. We turned right and climbed to only 13,000 feet, as the 747 cut through the clear air, crossed the coast overhead Malibu, and set course for the desert and Mojave. Numerous light aircraft populated the TCAS display, catching one last look at the end of an era.

To stay well clear, Ewen brought the 747 into a sweeping left orbit near Mojave airfield until the sky was empty once again. The turn afforded a spectacular view of the surrounding desert and the Providence Mountains to the east. Joining overhead, a visual circuit was flown, and finally, Runway 30 loomed ahead. The long black strip grew larger until Ewen finally eased Wunala to earth for the final time.

Aside from the mandatory checks and calls, the flight deck was quiet as the aircraft was taxied and parked in a line behind the three Qantas 747 sisters already in residence. The crew each took their turn at shutting down an engine and putting OEJ to bed for the final time. It was a special moment.

A tractor connected to Wunala's nose gear to tow her closer to the other 747s and we opened the hatch above the flight deck. From the best seat in the house, I climbed up and looked across the top of the aircraft, ahead towards the line of red fins and behind to the boneyard where a sea of aircraft was standing in the desert sun.

The media waited outside but as a crew, we gathered on the upper deck to have time to ourselves before the media rolled in. It was Ewen, Greg and possibly Sharelle's last flight and now it was over. We needed to share that.

In time, the media came on board, and we answered a range of questions fired at a rapid pace. The aviation blogger, Sam Chui, was among their number and kindly gave me a t-shirt that bore an old Qantas advertisement, featuring the 747. On the ground, we were met by more media beside the now silent 747, where they had Sharelle pose, seated within the engine cowl, recreating a shot from the start of her career.

Even in the excitement, it was impossible to ignore the sad sight of hundreds of scrapped airliner hulks on the far side of the airfield, knowing that was Wunala's fate. With formalities completed, we were driven to the boneyard and left to wander among the airframes. Tumbleweed blew past our feet and dust kicked up in the heat like a scene from an old western movie. However, there was no saloon or cowboys, just retired giants of the sky gradually being picked apart for their components, or skinned to create commemorative baggage tags.

Aircraft that had once rolled off the production line gleaming and arrived on flight lines to the warm welcome of airlines and passengers were now all but abandoned. Among their number, I spotted the original "Wunala," confirmed by "OJB" scrappily painted on a landing gear door beside the US registration it had used for its ferry flight from Victorville. There she sat, engines removed, doors missing, and the cargo holds open. Translucent plastic flapped in the wind where the First Officer's windscreen had once been fixed.

A short distance away, OJS was at rest. I had crewed her final sector to San Francisco eighteen months earlier before she was ferried to Mojave. We all climbed aboard, scrambling up a ladder beside the nosewheel and emerging through a hatch in the floor of business class. I wandered off and sadly examined the state she was in. Litter was strewn across the floor; old lifejackets were on seats and there were even blankets in open overhead lockers.

I climbed the stairs to the aft crew rest and onwards to the flight deck. I paused midway along the upper deck to film the scene using my phone when a loud "bang" came from the flight deck. On entering, the only possible cause that I could detect was that one of the emergency escape handles had freed itself from the roof and flung itself against the wall. Perhaps OJS was trying to tell me something.

On the flight deck, panels were missing from overhead, and wires hung down, their bayonet fittings still attached. Gaping holes existed where flight and engine instruments had once been. The seats had been removed and scraps of wire, plastic and washers covered the floor. A sad end for a once-proud girl.

We drove from the boneyard and past Wunala and her sisters towards the gate and onto the highway. As we exited the gate, I looked back one last time to see four proud red fins in formation. And then I looked away.

As the bus made the long trek to Manhattan Beach, the vehicle was almost silent. No doubt there was an element of fatigue involved but I suspect that it was something more – it certainly was for me.

At every opportunity, the media had asked, "How do you feel"? and "Are you emotional"? To be honest, we were task-focused, realising that the undertaking had the potential for errors, despite the immense preparation that had been undertaken. There was no time to be emotional, the job had to be done.

Still, as the vehicle rolled on, the desert landscape passed by as a blur. I looked around at the rest of the crew and suspected, like me, that this was the first time to reflect upon the flight. Those special moments - the kind words of an air traffic controller, the city of Sydney sweeping beneath our wings, the tears of staff as they waved us goodbye and those that had sung, "I still call Australia home."

It was the same feeling as we moved through the empty terminal at LAX to board the Delta Airlines flight home a day later. Spread out among business class, we were the sole inhabitants as we settled in for the night. A flight attendant came up to me and asked, "Are you the guys that drew the kangaroo"?

I nodded and smiled. "Yes, we were."

"That must have been amazing"!

I smiled again.

Yes, it was amazing.

And a farewell that I would never forget.

Sleep tight Wunala.

POSTSCRIPT

FAREWELL

FROM THE FLIGHT DECK.

It was not until I returned home from the flight that I appreciated how significant the final flight of Wunala had been. People from all over the planet messaged me through my website and social media, particularly regarding the sky art kangaroo.

As passionate as I was about aviation, aircraft remained inanimate objects. I wondered at their engineering and admired their lines but never particularly fell into the aircraft possessing a "heart and soul" philosophy that some believed in. Nor do most pilots. We are trained to be methodical and logical, rather than emotional. However, what the final flight and the writing of this book awakened in me were how aircraft and flight can stir these emotions.

As I retraced my personal 747 journey through the pages of this book, I came to realise that the aircraft had played a significant role in my life. When I was unemployed, it was the Boeing 747 that reignited my career. I may have been relegated to the Second Officer's seat through a twist of fate and the seniority system but as I consider this, it was a tremendous position to view the crew operate as a team and to observe the world around me.

When I needed a reprieve from domestic operations to focus on my family, it was the network of the 747 and Qantas that facilitated this. Not only did it afford us more time with our children, but it allowed us to show them places far beyond our borders.

Before the 747, I had not flown with Kirrily other than onboard a light aircraft from time to time and yet in my second term on the Jumbo, we were able to work together and then share wonderful memories of glaciers and the Golden Gate Bridge.

For so many people the 747 was associated with the happiest of memories. Family reunions, great adventures and family holidays were all brought alive when the door was closed, the aerobridge was retracted, and the Queen of the Skies pushed back for yet another flight. And the 747 did so with qualities that we relate to as human beings.

It was dependable, it was exciting, it was family and it had longevity, which is why its passing was felt by so many. It carried me across the world's most vast ocean, the frozen southern continent and the highest mountain ranges and never faltered – day or night, calm or storm. And the one occasion that we shut down a troubled engine, the 747 simply shrugged its shoulders and did what it was designed to do without a fuss.

The father of the Boeing 747, Joe Sutter, designed a fine aeroplane that was adapted over half a century and in the form of the 747-8 is still a magnificent machine. The four-engined giants may be fading from passenger operations, replaced by highly efficient, reliable twinjets. Still, the 747 will have a role to play in air freight for some years to come, thanks to its expansive volume and its upper deck.

In the end, the Boeing 747 was an engineering miracle that was ahead of its time. Millions of components, each honed with exact precision, created an aircraft for the ages. And yet it is still only alloy and oil, rivets, and fuel. However, it was the emotions that it evoked in those that flew her, flew on her, and even just admired her from a distance that made the aircraft so special. It was these emotions that made the Boeing 747 not just another aircraft – but the "Queen of the Skies".

About The Author.

Owen Zupp is a published author with more than 20,000 hours of varied flight experience and was fortunate to be one of the crew aboard the Qantas Boeing 747 final "Farewell Flight" to Los Angeles and the Mojave Air and Space Port. With more than 25 years in airline operations, Owen has flown both domestically and across the globe. He holds a Masters Degree in Aviation Management and his writings on aviation have been published around the world and received various accolades and awards.

The son of a decorated fighter pilot, Owen was born into aviation. His flying career has taken him from outback Australia to the rugged mountain ranges of New Guinea, the idyllic islands of Micronesia and across the oceans of the world. Whether witnessing rocket launches from 40,000 feet or circumnavigating a continent for charity in a tiny two-seat training aircraft, Owen has cherished every minute aloft. Flight is not merely his profession; it is his passion.

ACKNOWLEDGEMENTS.

There are always so many people to thank when a book is complete.

First and foremost, my wonderful wife, Kirrily, and our children, Ruby, Hannah, Beth and Hayden. They have had to endure both my absences due to flying and the long hours at the keyboard when I am home.

My dad both inspired me to fly and taught me to fly. He was the greatest father and role model that a young man could have.

To all of those that I have flown with, whether on short hops on sunny days in a biplane, or long nights bridging the Pacific. I have learned a little more each time that the wheels left the earth because of that time spent with you.

To Qantas and its people. Thank you for the support and opportunity to have made this amazing aviation journey possible.

To those readers of my first 747 book who insisted that I write this book. You were a bigger driving force than you will probably ever know.